Faith, Feminism, and the Christ

Faith, Feminism, and the Christ

PATRICIA WILSON-KASTNER

FORTRESS PRESS   Philadelphia

Library of Congress Cataloging in Publication Data

Wilson-Kastner, Patricia.
  Faith, feminism, and the Christ.

  Includes index.
    1. Feminism—Religious aspects—Christianity.
  2. Woman (Christian theology)   3. Jesus Christ—Person and
  offices.   I. Title.
  BT704.W54   1983   261.8'344   83–5688
  ISBN 0–8006–1746–0

127D83   Printed in the United States of America   1-1746

TO RONALD

My inestimable spouse and co-worker
Whose scholarship, support, and steady faith
have helped me dream and write this book,
and whose encouragement and enthusiasm
strengthen me for the future

Contents

Preface   ix

Introduction   1

1. A Feminist Critique: Humanity, Deity,
   the Christ   11

2. Another Way of Looking at the World   39

3. Feminism and Humanity   55

4. Roots of the Problem in Christology   71

5. Who Is This Christ?   89

6. The Trinity   121

Epilogue   139

Index of Names   143

Index of Scripture References   147

Preface

I wrote most of this book during a sabbatical leave from United Theological Seminary in the fall of 1982. Dr. Clyde Steckel, Academic Vice-President of the seminary, very kindly helped me arrange my schedule in the surrounding semesters so as to make best use of my time. During that fall I was a fellow at the College of Preachers at the National Cathedral in Washington, D.C., where the interim warden, the Rt. Rev. William Marmion, Dr. Earl Brill, the Rev. Barry Evans, and Masie Whitman were particularly helpful and supportive in the writing process. The Rev. Richard Deitch, William Phillips, and William Brewster, the other fellows, conversed, listened, and gave me confidence to continue this endeavor.

Thanks to a grant from the Association of Theological Schools during December 1982 I was able to travel to England to visit with people involved with the movement for the ordination of women in the Church of England, and also with persons active in feminist theology in Great Britain. Drs. Una Kroll, Mary Tanner, and Daphne Hampson, as well as Christian Howard, Daphne Frasier, and the Rev. Donald Reeves were particularly helpful and considerate of my needs.

Various good friends and colleagues have been subjected to conversations, arguments, discussions, and questions at various stages of the planning, dreaming, writing, and revising of this book. I am especially grateful to the Rev. Karen Smith Sellers and Dr. Mary F. Bednarowski of United Theological Seminary, who read and commented on the proposal for this book. Sr. Vera Chester, S.S.J., of the College of St. Catherine, Dr. Michael Slusser of the Catholic University of America, and Dr. Jane A. Boyajian of United Theological Seminary have constructively and helpfully criticized parts of the present manuscript. Professor David L. Balas, S.O. Cist., has over the years provided me with innumerable insights about Gregory of Nyssa and the vast resources of early theology which illuminate contemporary issues. I acknowledge and celebrate their contributions and insights, but must myself take responsibility for the weakness and omissions which remain.

In the final stages of revising the work, I was changing from United Theological Seminary to General Theological Seminary in New York City. Consequently, the typing of the manuscript moved from the care of Marian Hoeft and her staff at U.T.S. to the capable hands of Sandra Ley, faculty secretary at G.T.S. The library staff at U.T.S., especially Dr. Holt Graham and Harriet Kruse, and those at G.T.S., have been generous in their willingness to provide me with whatever resources I might need. Linda Strohmeier has generously assisted me in final revisions.

Biblical quotations, unless otherwise noted, are from the Revised Standard Version of the Bible. I have tried to employ quotations from the writers of the early and medieval churches using readily available sources, but have changed the translation as indicated to make the English more faithful to more inclusive language in the original.

I am especially grateful to Dr. John A. Hollar, Academic Editor at Fortress Press, whose patience, encouragement, meticulous attention, and useful suggestions have contributed immeasurably to the quality of this work. Above all, I am thankful to Dr. G. Ronald Kastner, my spouse and colleague in working toward an inclusive theology and practice in the church and in the world. Without his constant encouragement, criticism, and unfailing support, I would never have persevered to finish this work.

May 8, 1983
Feast of Julian of Norwich

> Patricia Wilson-Kastner
> Trinity Church Professor of Preaching
> The General Theological Seminary

Introduction

"But who do you say that I am?"

"You are the Christ, the Son of the living God."

Simon Peter was not the only person in history to have been confronted with that searching question, and his is not the only answer which has been given. Today people who consider themselves feminists must respond to the same query, both to the satisfaction of those radical or revolutionary feminists who pose the issue to them, and, more importantly, in accord with their own internal sense of rightness and equity.

Today some feminists insist that the only possible reply to Jesus' invitation is a rejection. Because explicit and implicit masculine language and imagery about God dominate in the Christian tradition, and because institutional Christianity almost since its beginning has justified the oppression of women, many feminists regard Christianity as an evil to be discarded. Mary Daly in *Beyond God the Father* and later in *Gyn/Ecology* and Naomi Goldenberg in *Changing of the Gods* articulate the fundamental position of revolutionary or counter-cultural feminists. They insist that both Judaism and Christianity are hopelessly patriarchal at their very foundations, and must be rejected by women who are seeking their own identities. Both Judaism and Christianity, they contend, deny women a whole and integrated self-concept, while obscuring for women the divine which is within them. Only a rejection of all patriarchal religion and the construction of new forms which arise from women's experience are acceptable as alternatives.[1]

In their anthology, *Womanspirit Rising*, Carol Christ and Judith Plascow explore some of the possibilities for contemporary alternatives to traditional religions. Some women advocate a return to worship of the mother goddess, often accompanied by a form of feminist witch-

1

craft. Others make humanity, especially women's sisterhood, their religious center; still others identify the individual with power within her as the key to a new religion.[2]

At the same time, while these radical or revolutionary feminists deny the possibility of any true rapprochement between feminism and Christianity, fundamentalist Christians deny that an authentic Christian can be a feminist. They assert that the Scriptures admit the spiritual equality of men and women, but in this world they belong to different spheres or worlds. Men are responsible for political, industrial, religious, and other forms of leadership activity. Women "belong" in the home and perhaps may pursue other related activities that nurture the family if they are supportive of and subordinate to men. Ordination to the ministry or to any other leadership position in which a woman would have authority over a man is forbidden.[3]

A variation on this argument, found mostly in Episcopal, Catholic, and Orthodox churches, is that the very maleness of Jesus argues against an equality of women and men in religious matters. In its extreme form, this line of reasoning asserts that humanity is "essentially binary; it exists only in the two modes of masculinity and femininity. . . . Under a difference of mode it [humanity] is essentially in each."[4] Because sexuality is assumed to be the essential distinguishing characteristic of the two modes of humanity, one can never assume that aspects of one form of humanity are transferable to another. Consequently, because Jesus was a male person, only male persons can be ordained, that is, be publicly recognized as worship leaders in a sacramental or mediating role.

Although one may hear versions of such language in papal pronouncements or conservative Anglo-Catholic circles, most theologians and religious leaders admit that theologically such arguments are inadequate; most frequently the opposition to women's ordination stems from practical and ecumenical concerns. The Orthodox are the only major community to sustain a vigorous theological denial of even the possibility of women's ordination and liturgical leadership.[5]

Biblical and doctrinal fundamentalists have squared off in battle against those who grant women full access to leadership in the church, while the revolutionary feminists deny the usefulness of church or the Christian notion of God. By contrast, most Christian women and men who are aware of the issues stand between the two, and wish to be both Christian and feminist with personal integrity. They seek ways to do so.

Although they understand and feel the cries from revolutionary feminists, nevertheless they still experience Christianity as the most helpful way of making sense out of the whole of their lives. Must they choose between Christianity and feminism?

During the last few years considerable energy and time have been devoted to this issue by people who wish to say that one does not need to give up one or the other. One can be *both* a feminist and a Christian, and *both* feminism and Christianity can contribute to each others' richness. On the level of religious and theological investigations, Christian feminist theologians have looked both to the past and the present which shape the future to explore some of the positive interrelationships possible between Christianity and feminism.

Some of these investigators have concentrated their energies on looking at the past relationship between Christianity and feminism. Recognizing that it is misleading to impose categories on the past, they acknowledge that often Christianity has allowed itself to be used to oppress women. This was true both in religious thought and theological systems, as well as in the actual social structure of the churches. Historians and biblical scholars of the stature of Joan Morris, Rosemary Radford Ruether, Phyllis Trible, and Eleanor McLaughlin have reexamined Christian religious history. In their research they have uncovered, along with the sad saga of repression, rich veins of the positive accomplishments of women in the history of the church. Increasingly, they are uncovering the nuances in the story of women in religion, discerning that the condition of women was different in diverse times and places and that a wide variety of factors has contributed to a complex tale filled with great as well as ordinary women whose struggles form a complex drama of high achievement.

Furthermore, along with scholars such as Raphael Patai and Leonard Swidler, they have brought to the fore the great riches of language and imagery in the theological traditions of Christianity that incorporate the feminine into representations of the divine. Thus they insist that a true picture of the relationship between feminism and Christianity in its past is far more complex than either fundamentalists or radical feminists would allow, and that the foundation for a more mature, just, equitable, and solid relationship between the two is rooted deeply in their emerging history.[6]

Another approach, related to that of those reconstructing the past, is that of people who in the light of their feminism wish to reconstruct

Christian theology in a way that would be meaningful to feminists and those who are faithful to the fundamental aim of Christianity. Letty Russell, Rosemary Radford Ruether, Marianne Micks, Sally McFague, and Joan Chamberlain Engelsman lead this effort to construct a new theology which will look afresh at the teachings and practice of the Christian tradition and suggest how feminist concerns will reshape it. Their efforts range from dealing with language about God to the ethical implications of the confinement of women to a "pink collar" ghetto. Scores of helpful books offer guidelines for applying more abstract thoughts to the realm of everyday practice.[7]

The achievements of these women and men are very real. The implications of their labors will continue to be felt in the disciplines of theology and the history of religions, as well as in applied disciplines such as spirituality, ethics, pastoral care, and liturgics. Their concern with god and/or goddess, imagery and theological connotations, tradition and contemporary possibilities will continue to be a source of discussion and fruitful interchange. Such explorations also fan the fire of conflict between persons who are trying to transform their traditions from within, and others who work for religious feminist forms that categorically reject Christianity.

But even after questions about the image of God and language about God have been adequately responded to, when the helpful dialogue is well under way, and after the past and present role of women in the church and society is explored in great depth with an eye toward a transformed future, a vexing problem remains for Christians. No matter how one analyzes, explains, and remythologizes, at the heart of the Christian faith lies Jesus Christ, a male human being.[8] In even the most minimal assessment, he is the moral teacher par excellence and the prime exemplification of the human being. For most Christians, he is the incarnate Lord, through whom God is made known to us. Jesus was certainly a male, and the male imagery attached to him cannot be explained away by recourse to the outmoded patriarchy of the biblical writers.

Even if our conceptions of God and the role of women in the church can be reinterpreted, the maleness of Jesus would appear to be an insuperable barrier to a feminist seeking an inclusive or "depatriarchalized" figure at the core of religion. Naomi Goldenberg deals with the challenge most bluntly:

Jesus Christ cannot symbolize the liberation of women. A culture that maintains a masculine image for its highest divinity cannot allow its women to experience themselves as the equals of its men. In order to develop a theology of women's liberation, feminists have to leave Christ and the Bible behind them.[9]

But what if a feminist still wishes to be a Christian because that person finds within Christianity, despite its sexism and oppression, the strength of a truth which overcomes even its own limits to bring life and freedom to the seeker? Must that feminist also leave Christ and the Bible behind to find true freedom and fulfillment? The *aim* of my work is to explore the significance of these questions, and to suggest that the most fundamental meaning of Christ for Christianity is that of reconciliation and inclusiveness. True as it may appear that certain forms of Christianity and feminism are mutually incompatible, such does not need to be the case. Insights and questions of feminism can illumine and correct Christology, and an adequate Christology can enrich the feminism of any feminist who seeks a living Christianity.

Despite the importance of the interrelationship between feminism and Christology, few overtures of this kind have been made.[10] Unhappily, both feminists who reject Christianity and those who accept it suffer from that omission. Those who reject Christ and Christianity often do so from historically inadequate knowledge and an overly simplistic notion about the image of Christ in present Christian theologies and throughout the ages. Christian feminists sometimes miss or are unaware of insights from the tradition which could enrich their own understanding of Christ and his liberating significance for women as well as men.

I openly admit that my whole endeavor is meaningful only if one is convinced that an immanent/transcendent Deity is a proper focus for the religious quest, and that Christianity has much light to cast on that search. Anyone who is unwilling to admit at least such possibilities will probably become impatient with my efforts. One who is not a feminist will find the whole exercise unnecessary. But any feminist, woman or man, who believes that humanity finds its fulfillment only through an encounter with the divine which interprets and gives shape to all other experience will find this attempt useful, even though she or he may disagree with specific contentions of mine.

The fundamental conviction of the compatibility, or at least the noncontradictory relationship, between Christianity and feminism underlies the whole of this book. I hold other fundamental assumptions, some of which may not be so apparent. I think it only fair of me to warn the reader. They all relate to my approach to doing theology and the way in which I think it appropriate to raise theological issues and relate them to feminism.

My assumptions are as follows:

1. Theology and religious faith are not the same. Religious faith constitutes a fundamental personal relationship to the sacred. Faith may be expressed in a variety of physical, emotional, or intellectual ways, but they all spring from a primary, suprarational acceptance of the divine, rooted in a sense of the presence of the Ultimate to the self. Theology is the rational spelling-out and explaining of one's faith. There are many possible explanations, even for the same individual, and therefore many possible theologies. These theologies are influenced by point of view, questions raised by the individual and the culture of which the person is a part, the intellectual framework of the person formulating the theology, and so forth. Theology is a superstructure which arises from a faith, and expresses it on one significant but limited level. In this book, my primary focus is on theology, not on the faith which feeds it.

2. If one were to search among other human acts for a comparison to the activity of faith, the best would be, I think, aesthetic experience. Insight, intuition, creativity, and appreciation—each has its analogue in a faith which both apprehends and feels itself grasped by the divine, reaches new depths of itself and others, and enjoys the beauty of all in light of the Ultimate.[11] Theology, in this case, is most comparable to activities like aesthetics, or art or literary criticism. It is a limited, modest, always inadequate, but absolutely essential endeavor to explain intellectually what beauty is, how it is present in and to us, and how we realize it. Thus any attempt to "prove" theology or faith is foolhardy. At the same time, to claim that any faith is perfect or any theology the final or full answer is as absurd as the notion that any artist has perfectly apprehended or expressed all beauty.

3. I accept the idea, at the core of the classical Christian tradition, that God is both immanent and transcendent. Those terms have been maligned at different times and places throughout religious history. In the present time, many feminists who are interested in religion find the notion of divine transcendence oppressive and expressive of the male

patriarchy; their arguments will be considered later. My understanding of God as immanent/transcendent views these terms as efforts to account for a God who is at one and the same time holy, inexpressible, and greater than all that is, and also is One whom all creation resembles, and who is present in and to all creation. Thus I am operating with a different notion of God and interpretation of classical Christianity than those who would suggest God is the "totally other," different from and unknowable to creation, or those who would understand God as completely or partially identical with the created world.

4. When I refer to Christology I mean theological and rational explanations of Jesus Christ. I am not referring directly to an experience of Christ or faith in Christ, although those are experiences at the root of Christology and must be taken into account. In the Christian tradition, Jesus Christ is the focus or prism through whom God is known and interpreted to the Christian community. This is not necessarily a claim that Christ is the only revelation of God (for a variety of reasons I regard that claim as shortsighted and wrong) but I do insist that God is manifest to us in Christ and that in the Christian tradition we take the figure of Christ—the revelation of God—as the one through whom we interpret other revelations, other understandings of God, the world, and ourselves. Christ signifies the historical figure of Jesus—the one through whom God is made known to us—as well as the living Christ of Word and Sacrament in the church throughout the ages.

Besides explaining some fundamental assumptions of the book, I must also acknowledge an awareness of some feminists who protest the very notion of writing a book about feminist theology. Today there is indeed a strong sentiment among many feminists, who regard themselves as community- and experience-centered, against any attempt at abstract, intellectual presentations which conform to male-dominated academic models. I admit a well-known tendency in academic circles to mistake clear and tidy discussions for reality and to so refine and reify knowledge that the mental product appears to have very little to do with the existing reality. Unquestionably males also have had a stronghold on academic thinking and have often forced themselves and the women who inhabit academe to express themselves in uselessly pedantic forms. But I believe that there is nothing exclusively male or female about clear thinking about personal experience. Our primary concern must always be that our thinking *and* our experience constantly interact with each other and with the human community of thought and experience. Only thus can females and males communicate with themselves and with each other and grow in appreciation and insight about the world and themselves as equal partners. To write a book is an act of faith in that process of growth; it is one modest act in the infinitely greater process of humanity's development.

Because theological efforts of the sort I am suggesting are so new, I have not written an academic book in the ordinary sense of the word. Although there are footnotes, and theologians of the past provide insights essential to my work, for the most part I have focused on major ideas and themes. I have searched for a vision; therefore I have not specified all my sources and spelled out every possible implication of my proposal.

I have attempted to reconstruct Christology and its fundamental concerns in the light of feminist values. Consequently I have begun with the radical critique that the feminist movement makes of a Christian understanding of the human condition, God, and Christ. In the perspective of its challenges and questions I have tried to outline a constructive theological response. I have tried to articulate a vision of humanity, God, and Christ that is both an expression of the Christian community's experience of Christ, and also explicitly responsive to feminist concerns.

NOTES

1. Mary Daly, *Beyond God the Father* (Boston: Beacon Press, 1973) and *Gyn/Ecology* (Boston: Beacon Press, 1978); Naomi Goldenberg, *The Changing of the Gods* (Boston: Beacon Press, 1979).

2. Carol Christ and Judith Plascow, *Womanspirit Rising* (New York: Harper & Row, 1979), 1–17, 193–287; Christ explores some of these themes further in *Diving Deep and Surfacing: Women Writers on Spiritual Quest* (Boston: Beacon Press, 1980). Penelope Washbourn's *Becoming Woman* (New York: Harper & Row, 1977) provides an example of a new tradition explicitly based on woman's physical-psychological experience; Starhawk's *The Spiral Dance* (New York: Harper & Row, 1979) provides an example of a tradition based on women's religion as witchcraft.

3. Susan T. Fob, in *Women and the Word of God* (Grand Rapids: Baker Book House, 1979) expounds a biblically conservative version of this argument, insisting that women are ontologically equal to men, but subordinate in the economy of salvation.

4. Eric L. Mascall, "Some Basic Considerations," in *Man, Woman, Priesthood,* ed. Peter Moore (London: SPCK, 1978), 21.

5. Michael Bruce and G.E. Duffield, eds., *Why Not? Priesthood and the Ministry of Women* (Appleford, Eng.: Marchham Manor Press, 1972) includes essays opposing women's ordination from a wide variety of perspectives. Emily Hewitt and Suzanne R. Hiatt's *Women Priests: Yes or No* (New York: Seabury Press, 1973) summarizes arguments on both sides, and Paul K. Jewett, *The Ordination of Women* (Grand Rapids: Wm. B. Eerdmans, 1980) classifies and refutes arguments against women's ordination and assumption of leadership roles. The literature about women's ordination provides a useful focus for attitudes toward women's functioning in the institutional church, vehicles through which the feminine images and language are used to express the divine, and processes through which the Scriptures and tradition are reinterpreted. Pope John Paul II's new encyclical *Exercens laborem* assumes a distinctive "women's nature," complementary to male nature, and discusses this within an official Roman Catholic ecclesiastical framework.

6. Leonard Swidler, "Jesus Was a Feminist," *Catholic World* 212 (January 1971): 177–83 and *Biblical Affirmations of Women* (Philadelphia: Westminster Press, 1979); Joan Morris, *The Lady Was A Bishop* (New York: Macmillan Co., 1973); Raphael Patai, *The Hebrew Goddess* (New York: Avon Books, 1967, 1978); Rosemary Radford Ruether and Eleanor McLaughlin, eds., *Women of Spirit* (New York: Simon & Schuster, 1979); Rosemary Radford Ruether, ed., *Religion and Sexism* (New York: Simon & Schuster, Touchstone Books, 1974) (both of the Ruether anthologies contain relevant studies by Barbara Brown Zikmund, Eleanor McLaughlin, and others); Phyllis Trible, *God and the Rhetoric of Sexuality,* Overtures to Biblical Theology (Philadelphia: Fortress Press, 1978).

7. The most helpful of Ruether's works which deals generally with feminism and theology is *New Women and New Earth* (New York: Seabury Press, 1975). Also helpful are Letty Russell, *Human Liberation in a Feminist Perspective—A Theology* (Philadelphia: Westminster Press, 1974); Joan Chamberlain Engelsman, *The Feminine Dimension of the Divine* (Philadelphia: Westminster Press, 1979); Marianne H. Micks, *Our Search for Identity: Humanity in the Image of God* (Philadelphia: Fortress Press, 1982); Marianne Sawicki, *Faith and Sexism* (New York: Seabury Press, 1979); Erminie Huntress Lantero, *Feminine Aspects of Divinity* (Wallingford, Pa.: Pendle Hill Publications, 1973). Susan Dowell and Linda Hurcombe's *Dispossessed Daughters of Eve* (London: SCM Press, 1981) pulls together practical and theoretical issues within an English context.

8. Ninian Smart, *In Search of Christianity* (San Francisco: Harper & Row, 1979), 201.

9. Goldenberg, *Changing of the Gods,* 22.

10. Engelsman, in *Feminine Dimension,* 151–53, briefly reflects on some of the history of the relationship between the idea of Christ and that of Sophia, a relationship which might introduce some feminine imagery into the notion of

the divine in contemporary theology. Rosemary Radford Ruether's *To Change the World: Christology and Cultural Criticism* (New York: Crossroad, 1981) deals specifically with Christology and feminism, pp. 45–56.

11. In the complex debate about whether or not one may properly speak of a specifically aesthetic attitude or experience, I am asserting that one may. For an introduction to this issue, see the essays by Jerome Stolnitz and Georgie Dickie, with the appended reading list, in *Introductory Reading in Aesthetics,* ed. John Hospers (New York: Free Press, 1969), 17–45.

CHAPTER 1

A Feminist Critique:
Humanity, Deity, the Christ

NAMING THE ISSUES

Before attempting to construct a feminist reinterpretation of theology, it is appropriate to examine with care the main lines of feminist thinking on issues crucial to Christology. I have identified three areas as being central for our efforts: epistemology, that is, how we know; the nature of the divine; and who Christ is. In attempting to gain new insight, I have examined feminist positions that are significant to the feminist community, in my opinion, and especially those whose arguments have influenced my own thoughts and opinions.

How Do Women Know?

This topic would appear to be self-evident and clear; it is not. In my own constructive chapter I will outline a few reasons why I think that this is an intrinsically interesting and necessary question, but here I will point to a few pragmatic reasons. The opinions of many feminists on this question are linked to certain strong notions as to whether or not men and women share the same human nature, or are fundamentally different. Our response to this concern becomes especially significant because one's understandings of our common humanity or lack thereof affect the ways we perceive the divine and our relationship to it.

Among those who have written about women's way of knowing, there are two major divisions. One upholds a uniquely woman's way of apprehending the world, and the other maintains that knowing is essentially a human activity, and therefore one cannot speak of any unique way in which women have knowledge.

Many contemporary feminists, especially the self-styled radical or revolutionary feminists, would insist that women are human beings of quite a different sort from men. Therefore the way they know is quite

11

distinct from the way men know. Some feminists work from a philosophical base, and others from a psychological starting point, but they unite in their insistence on the uniqueness of the female, and often on its superiority to the male.

In *Beyond God the Father,* and later in *Gyn/Ecology,* Mary Daly has developed a theory about the uniqueness of a female way of knowing. Beginning with her rejection of not only male superiority but also the notion that women should retain anything of male ways of knowing the world or expressing that knowledge, Daly insists that a woman's understandings must emerge from her own understandings and experiences and her attempts to put those into words.

> To exist humanly is to name the self, the world, and God. The "method" of evolving spiritual consciousness of women is nothing less than this beginning to speak humanly—a reclaiming of the right to name. The liberation of language is rooted in the liberation of ourselves.[1]

For women to become fully themselves, Daly claims, they must get in touch with the true women-self which has been suppressed by the patriarchy, and their consciousness must be liberated from the methods and the thoughts into which men have forced their experiences and insights.

She asserts that humanity has been divided into two halves by the patriarchy which rules society. The authority figure is "the eternal masculine"—hyperrational, objective, one who manipulates the world, inclusive of the environment and other persons, and sets up boundaries between the self and the other. This dominant masculine figure depends for his power on the existence of the "eternal feminine"—the emotional, passive one who does not seek to know, understand, and comprehend others or the world about her.[2]

In *Beyond God the Father* Daly advocates an androgyny of the person, the blending of traditional masculine and feminine characteristics in every human being. Because of the present state of their oppression, women must leave the society in which men and women live together, and belong exclusively to the sisterhood of the oppressed in order to discover who they are and how they know. In *Gyn/Ecology* she insists that the true women are those who are woman-centered. Only those women who are no longer dependent on men to tell them what or how to be in the world and who do not rely on men for any sort of personal or professional companionship are truly women.[3] Lesbian separatism is the appropriate style of living for women, the only one in which they can be truly human.

For Daly, whether women and men can be equally human is an increasingly irrelevant question. In fact, men are oppressive and at best will allow some women, who are willing to accept the conditions of servitude, to gain admittance to their little clubs. For a woman to do so is to accept the negation of her true personhood, her sisterhood, which is radically different from male, death-oriented bonding. Women must accept and nurture the uniqueness of their own experiences by boldly uttering what they have known and felt. They must bond themselves to other women, in a life-giving field of force that is radically different from that of patriarchal service of death. They must spin their "cosmic tapestries" through their own listening and discovery, and celebrate the depth of life within the world and themselves.[4]

Carol P. Christ explores this question of the way women perceive reality in *Diving Deep and Surfacing*. She suggests that as a woman theologian she learned that *because she was a woman* she did have a different perspective on theology, one which her male colleagues and professors found to be inferior to their own. Christ characterizes her approach as an aesthetic and poetic one, different from the male mode of theologizing.[5]

From Christ's perspective, women cannot even speak with confidence of their way of apprehending the world because they have not been able to utter their own stories, through which they could articulate their experience, examine it, say what they think of it, speak of its effect on them, and of what they like and what changes they wish to make. Both in theology and, more importantly, in storytelling, women either have not been allowed to tell their stories or have only used the forms of storytelling that a male-dominated society has imposed on them. Because women have not been able to tell their stories in their own ways, they do not really understand their own experience.

Through her survey of the literary output of female writers who have articulated their experiences as women Christ identifies several characteristics of a woman's way of experiencing and understanding the world. "Mystical awakenings through nature" give a woman a sense of the power within her. Through her sense of the power of nature within her she can begin the new naming of self and the world which results in a new knowing, a new and previously inaccessible perception of the world. Christ identifies the drive for wholeness and the integration of spiritual and social quests as dimensions of this experience.[6]

In this search for an experience of the power within, Christ emphasizes the importance of the woman's body as the medium by which she has had contact with the world and is able to integrate her sense of self with being at one with the world. Important in the expression and nurturing of this sense of wholeness and contact with the power of life is the creation of new rituals in which women can share their experiences, recognize them, name, and claim them as their own—as women.

Carol Christ focuses on the issue of the relationship of woman with nature in a woman's quest for spiritual wholeness. She acknowledges that some feminists, such as Judith Plaskow, object to too much emphasis being placed on the connection between women and nature, suggesting that such an approach can reinforce age-old patriarchal stereotypes about women and biological determinism. Christ argues, however, that women (and even men) need to develop new understandings of the body and its connections with nature, a reintegration of their connections with nature and the human ability to control it. Christ sees this emphasis on the woman's body and its connection with nature to be the first stage in a movement toward a holistic way of thinking.[7]

Christ does not claim that women and men, freed from cultural strictures, would know reality differently, but she insists that in the present order of things women do in fact experience themselves and the world differently. She implies that although both men and women are capable of a holistic way of experiencing the world, nevertheless, at this stage of the world's development women have had the opportunity to experience reality in ways that are more holistic than the male's dichotomized, dualistic way.

Penelope Washbourn and Ann Belford Ulanov explore further this claim of a unique female experience of the world. Washbourn acknowledges the healing significance of an insight gained from a Jungian therapist: "The uniqueness of my female identity and the spiritual value of my own self [could only be understood by me] as a continuous journey in life, through many modes of self-expression and self-encounter."[8] In *Becoming Woman* Washbourn sets out her intention to analyze "life crises" of women according to Erik Erikson's theories of personality development and Richard Rubenstein's theories of the need for religious rituals to mark times of personal passage. Because

Washbourn believes that religious questions and insights emerge during times of crisis, she seeks her understanding of what it is to be women in terms of the female developmental process.

She describes each of the life-passages of a woman: menstruation (especially menarche, but also each recurring episode), leaving home, sexual maturity (first sexual intercourse), love, failure and loss, marriage, pregnancy and birth, parenthood, the change of life (menopause), and the anticipation of death. Through these changes and stages women are constantly developing, and thus there is no static woman-herself. At the same time, for Washbourn, the development of the whole self depends on the self emergent from the biological process and the way one reflects on and accepts one's place in the whole of life. In a very real sense, a woman's way of perceiving, experiencing, and interpreting life is fundamentally different from a man's because it depends on her female body. Different women experience their bodies in varied ways. But because the basic insights and most fundamental experiences are in, through, and because of their female bodies, women's experience will always be radically different from men's experience, which is based on their own biological identity. Washbourn is one the clearest exponents of the idea of a uniquely female way of experiencing the world and the self because of one's physical makeup.

On the basis of Jungian psychological assumptions, Ann Belford Ulanov insists that "the Female has her own way of being and cannot be defined from a male or pseudo-male point of view."[9] In *Receiving Woman* Ulanov outlines the uniquely female way of being. For Ulanov "receiving" is the metaphor that best summarizes the uniqueness of being woman. The physical experience of giving birth is the key experience that expresses woman's possibilities:

> Literal birth-giving is paradigmatic for all kinds of metaphorical birth-giving in the creative arts, in intense love, and in religious experience. We learn in all of these to yield to a will which moves in us but is not our own, that does not snuff out our own will, but moves ours strongly into accord with its own. Such an experience marks us forever. . . . Women realize this will at an instinctual level. . . . To know she possesses personal access, in her own body, to this experience of cooperation with a life force beyond her control, gives a woman a special spiritual potential.[10]

Ulanov rejects three perceptions of the relation of male to female: the polarization of sex roles; the annihilation of sexual polarity; and the attempt to develop an androgynous human being. She insists that androgyny—the ideal human as equally incorporating male and female characteristics—must be rejected in favor of an acceptance of the various ways of being woman. For Ulanov there are various aspects of being woman; one of them is the motherly "receiving" and nurturing of life; another the "receiving" and incorporating into the self of the *animus*— the male principle or contrasexual factor. For women the *animus* is the bridge to the unconscious through which the woman incorporates the masculine side of her psyche into the feminine self.[11]

Instead of basing her arguments for the uniqueness of woman primarily on her bodily experience, as does Washbourn, Ulanov focuses on her psychological characteristics. She asserts that the woman who unites her personal feelings and values with her assumptions, convictions, and attitudes is able to personalize the world around her with a "strong life-giving warmth."[12] According to Ulanov, woman's being must be centered in its unique core, her receiving and nurturing. Although she acknowledges and defends the womanhood of the childless woman, the primary definition of woman is as mother because the woman both perceives the world and receives it as mother. Therefore she knows the world by identifying with it, by being-with-it, as the mother knows her child by being with, receiving, and nurturing the child which is hers. Consequently women must accept this mode of knowing and acknowledge it as uniquely theirs. If they accept their character as women, then their unique contribution to theology and religion will be their vulnerability, their weakness, their willingness to accept the negative in others and in themselves into the core of their beings, to rejoice with others, and to heal.[13]

Besides these feminists, one from a philosophical base and one from a psychological base, who would insist on the essential differences between the ways in which men and women know, there are also those who underline the common humanity of men and women in their ways of knowing the world. Carol Heilbrun, in *Toward a Recognition of Androgyny* and *Reinventing Womanhood,* proposes as her model for humanity androgyny, the incorporation of so-called masculine and feminine characteristics into each human person. In the latter work, she clarifies the woman's task today:

> They [women] must have a stronger psychological base, a wider foothold, than can be provided by female experience alone. The reinvention of

womanhood, I think, requires chiefly an effort to widen its boundaries and enlarge its scope. If women can take as their own the creative possibilities, the human aspirations once the property of men only, can they not also adopt male role models in their struggle for achievement? I believe that women must learn to appropriate for their own use the examples of human autonomy and self-fulfillment displayed to us by the male world.[14]

Through a careful analysis of literature by both women and men she demonstrates her contention that the experience of women has been underrated and often not appreciatively evaluated, even by women authors. She concludes, therefore, that women must be able to exercise their humanity in expanding their possibilities to encompass the full range of human experience, and not remain confined within the restricted limits which they have been given by male-dominated cultures.

She points to the American and French feminist theories that women and men are two distinct, irrevocably different kinds of human beings. The American psychological theory she rejects, but the French linguistically based theory she finds intriguing because of its imaginative possibilities. Following Jacques Lacan and Jacques Derrida, the structuralist literary critics, French feminists analyze language and male history and find them exhausted. They believe that women must express their own female experiences and apprehensions of the world in a new language, women's language. This French theory attracts Carol Heilbrun because it invites women to imagine, to reconstruct language and culture.[15]

Heilbrun clearly does not assert an unequivocal separation of male and female human beings; she does insist that humanity itself requires its full self-development through women's development, incorporating into their lives, thought, and activities a fullness of experience and imagination which has not yet been allowed. Following Simone de Beauvoir, she asserts that there are humans and women, and when women attempt to become human they are accused of being unwomanly. Heilbrun encourages women to become human because she assumes that they are human in the same fundamental sense as men are.

Letty M. Russell, in *Human Liberation in a Feminist Perspective* and *The Future of Partnership,* rejects the notion that women and men are two separate kinds of human beings. In the first work she advocates "humanization" as the goal of the search for equality. Acknowledging the different understandings of the human, she suggests that any notion of humanity must center on relational characteristics: love, freedom, and respect. That is, humans find themselves and are fully human in communities where they are supported, in which they are able to participate in shaping the common life and in which they are accepted as human subjects. She groups together women and Third World persons as ones who seek this kind of humanity, in which their capabilities and their achievements are not labeled "woman's" or "black" but are accepted as human.[16]

In discussing humanization she speaks about various ways in which men and women can exercise their partnership in serving God and cooperate in the transformation of the world into that in which God has intended both to live. Russell rejects, however, the arbitrary cultural roles and expectations imposed on women. She advocates the transformation of the "woman's" problem into the "human" problem. Following the work of sociologist Alice Rossi, she advocates a model for interaction between males and females in which psychological and cultural expectations about women's roles are rejected, and women and men develop their capabilities and gifts together according to their several human capacities.[17]

In *The Future of Partnership,* Russell expounds her understanding of partnership as the proper relationship between persons on a one-to-one basis, in local communities, churches, or on a global scale. She rejects attempts to discern any distinction between woman and man in the Genesis accounts and opposes the notion of "androgyny" used by some feminists (because it connotes dualism). She insists that partnership is fundamentally an eschatological notion; it urges us on to become what we can become. Consequently any preconceptions or predetermined notions are to be thoroughly rejected. Partnership involves the working and living together in the world by human beings whose roles are not preordained simply because of sex, but whose capabilities and gifts ought to be allowed to flourish in cooperation with each other.[18]

No tidy, uniform synthesis is possible among these different approaches. Russell and Ulanov, both committed feminists, differ almost completely in their understanding of the relation between humanity and women and in their analysis of how women perceive the world and interpret it. Some feminists search for an androgynous vision of the human, others for a biologically or psychologically based definition of woman which would radically distinguish her from male human beings. Some attempt to describe woman on the basis of her own experiences, while others insist on the essential identity between female and male humanness. Clearly, there is no agreed-upon feminist orthodoxy about the essential definition of woman or her way of knowing.

Rather than attempt a comparison and contrast of these varying views, I will highlight two common themes that emerge from these various feminist writings. Later I will develop further my own approach to an epistemology for feminist theology. From these diverse approaches to the way that women know a consensus has formed: feminists are convinced that women have been restricted in the past by the ways they have been allowed to experience the world and express that experience. Those who claim an intrinsic and fundamental difference between males and females and those who deny it both maintain that the emotional and intellectual growth of women has been truncated and restricted because of external limits society has placed on women. They have been confined and restricted to participation in a world which men have been able to know and experience more fully. Feminists therefore advocate either the self-development and self-expression of women as human beings in as full a way as men have been permitted, or the incorporation within their unique womanhood of the good qualities which men have been able to actualize.

Both of these approaches assume that any epistemology acceptable to women must have as its primary goal the quest for wholeness: the apprehension of the self, other selves, and everything which we experience in the world as intrinsically interrelated, forming an interdependent interconnected system that can only be fully understood and appreciated as one overarching reality. Feminists agree that women seek to know themselves and the world more fully. In other words, they are trying to know the whole rather than just a part. Carol Christ and others explicitly make the notion of wholeness the center of their understanding of women's spiritual quest.[19] Feminists also insist that they aim for a wholeness which is in the process of realization. From various perspectives, they acknowledge that the world is growing and developing toward a fullness that no one can yet describe. Feminists do not claim to have a road map of how the world is growing toward wholeness, but all would maintain that these developments are taking place.

Among Christian feminists one can also discern two other characteristics. God or the divine is an essential aspect of the wholeness that women seek and the wholeness that is desired. As Rosemary Radford Ruether has observed, Christian feminism must also reject any sort of fundamental separation or essential distinction between women and men. Differences there may be, but there are not women's and men's reality, women's and men's religion. Human reality is one, and human wholeness emerges from the development of the whole of humanity, without the obstacles of preconceptions and stereotypes.[20]

All feminists share some common framework of reference. Feminist theology must be developed in awareness of those characteristics of feminist epistemology, with a consciousness that *any* epistemology must deal with the whole as well as parts: how do we perceive the totality, what are the interconnections among all the various parts of the world, and what is the whole in which and into which the world is developing?

God or Goddess?

Even though I focus primarily on Christology in this book, I must briefly comment on the debate about the notion of God in contemporary feminism. The link between Christ and God is an obvious theological issue. Feminists have constructed visions of the divine that have a direct or indirect application to any Christology that takes feminism seriously. Therefore I will attend to major feminist notions about the divine and give a brief sketch of divine reality from my own constructive position.

To refer to "God" in certain feminist circles is sometimes perceived as a hostile act, or at best one emerging from ignorance. "God" is interpreted as a patriarchal deity who was and still is envisaged by his adherents as male, and who supports the male-dominated patriarchy. Even when religious systems protest that they believe God is "without body, parts, or passions," many feminists claim that the inevitable use of the pronoun "he" for this deity ensures that people still imagine and really believe that this God is male. The perception of feminists is sometimes supported by learned members of the religious community who cannot be accused of clinging to mere naive folk religion. For instance, Gilbert Russell and Margaret Dewey claim: "If then God, as Christians are bound to encounter and to envisage him, has to be male, that fact must bear on the ordination of women."[21] Because such a belief, even if subliminal, still persists, deity and maleness are linked quite directly. Such opponents of women's equality treat maleness as normative humanity in the divine image, affirming femaleness as good only as much as it is like maleness. Because woman can never be a male, woman is implied or directly stated to be inferior, because she is not as perfect an image of the divine as the male. This oppressive masculine language and imagery is used by the patriarchy to enforce various social structures and a religious inferiority complex among women.

Although feminists agree that the meaning of "God" and language about the divine are important, they have responded differently to the same problem. One group rejects speaking of God as Ultimate Reality, and uses the term Goddess, either to designate the divine or to express the power within women. Others reinterpret the notion of God to make "it" as nonsexist as possible, understanding it as a genderless or androgynous label, regarding the "Goddess" as drawing attention to its sex-relatedness.

Those who worship the Goddess, whether the theorists or the more practically concerned, defend this religion and are loathe to be specific about what they mean. They do not wish to be too intellectual, deeming that as one of the great failings of the patriarchy. They also share a commitment to the liberation of women which is to be realized through participation in Goddess worship: for some a religious act, for others a psychological or political act, or all three. Carol Christ separates three responses made by various women to questions about who or what the Goddess is:

> (1) The Goddess is divine female, a personification who can be invoked in prayer and ritual; (2) the Goddess is symbol of the life, death, and rebirth energy in nature and culture, in personal and communal life and (3) the Goddess is symbol of the affirmation of the legitimacy and beauty of female power.[22]

As Christ also notes, these three categories often overlap, and specific feminists may accept one, two, or all three of these perceptions.[23]

Some feminists clearly claim that the Goddess is essentially a symbol for the self-affirmation of women, either individually or as the "sisterhood." The most overt assertion is made by Naomi Goldenberg. She contends that feminists are bringing an end to God, and she rejoices over that, partly because she finds the idea of God repressive to women, and also because she "had no great tie to God anyway. He never seemed to be relevant to me at all."[24] She criticizes various feminists who are searching for a meaningful notion of God that is in accord with their feminism. In her own response she acknowledges an acceptance of Freud's criticism of religion as rooted in a man's obsession with the father figure magnified into god, making religion into the most repres-

sive institution in modern Western culture. Because Freud's insight into
the repressiveness of patriarchal religion is correct, she concludes, if
modern women are to develop into healthy and whole human beings,
Yahweh and Christ must die.[25]

Because she assumes, with Freud, that God is an internal force, his
death is essential for women's liberation, as is the birth of new symbols
which will sustain them in their freedom. For Goldenberg, psychology
reveals to us the truth that "all myths . . . have their bases in the mind
and should never be credited with a reality independent of the mind."[26]
What women need, therefore, is a mythic system to enable them to
affirm the power within themselves. Psychology provides them with
that system.[27]

Goldenberg praises witchcraft highly because in the practical realm it
locates divinity within the woman's self. Its characteristics such as
women regarding themselves as divine, the Goddess as more important
than the male God, women's creation of their own rituals, all give
women a sense of being powerful and valuable, not dependent on or
inferior to males. Through worship of the Goddess as a symbol women
free themselves to feel the force and capability within them.

Carol Christ accepts a similar view, seeing the primary value of the
Goddess as a symbol, although she would not exclude any of the
possible interpretations of the Goddess as "wrong." She outlines the
various ways the symbol of the Goddess functions: (1) as affirmation
of women's trust in their power and that of other women in family and
society; (2) as affirmation of woman's body and the "life cycle
expressed in it"; (3) as a positive valuation of women's will and personal self-determination; (4) as reevaluation of women's "bonds and
heritage."[28]

In a similar way she describes the Goddess: "It is a new naming of
women's power, women's bodies, women's feelings of connection to
nature, and women's bonds with each other."[29] Christ expresses inter-
est in the Goddess as a symbol for power within women individually
and women bonded together. At the same time she disclaims any sense
of obligation to the Goddess in history, approaching the religion of the
Goddess only as a contemporary issue about the Goddess' function for
women. Women should feel free to use the Goddess as a symbol of that
which is best in them. Christ regards that as an appropriate way to
understand the Goddess. Any attempt to be more precise might cause
division among women, a possibility Christ wishes to avoid.[30]

Others active in the witchcraft movement assert that to speak of the

Goddess involves significant psychic intensity: the Goddess is the symbol through which we gain access to our secret selves, to those aspects of the female which have been lost through history or through cultural forces repressing them. Starhawk, for instance, emphasizes that witchcraft is "a religion of poetry, not theology,"[31] and therefore she does not attempt to press for clear and precise definitions. At the same time, she writes much about the Goddess, and clearly defines her as more than a power within the individual and among women.

Starhawk insists: "The symbolism of the Goddess is not a parallel structure to the symbolism of God the Father. The Goddess does not rule the world; She *is* the world."[32] The world is a manifestation of the Goddess. The Goddess is the Mother and the Power which brings us in and out of existence, which is present in everything and everywhere, in ourselves and in love of ourselves and others.[33]

Starhawk insists that the Goddess in witchcraft exists both "as psychological symbol and as manifest reality. . . . She exists *and* we create her."[34] Though vaguely expressed it appears that Starhawk understands witchcraft to worship the Goddess as a pantheistic force. The Goddess is the flow of life who is the sum of all that lives, but also a life force surging within all that is to bring it into being and to receive it into death, and witchcraft affirms these beliefs.

Mary Daly's thought about the divine falls into "early post-Christian" and "late post-Christian" stages. In her earlier work, *Beyond God the Father*, she writes of God the Verb, who is not the Father, Son, or Mother. This divine power somewhat resembles Paul Tillich's "Ground of Being," a divine power present in all reality as its source, and communicating life, movement, and reality to us.[35] Daly spends little time interpreting her notion of God the Verb, but uses this idea of the divine reality to validate the power within women and their communities. *Gyn/Ecology* contains no mention of God the Verb, and little discussion of the Goddess. She laments the primordial event of the "dismembering of the Goddess," whom she describes as "the deep Source of creative integrity in women."[36] The Goddess finally seems to be reduced to a functional term for the political consciousness-raising of women, which bonds them together.

New Directions in Understanding God

Some feminists do not wish to change present theological and religious expressions about God, either because they believe they allow adequate scope for women's needs in seeking freedom, or because they think that recovering some of the lost traditions can supply what is needed with relatively little reform of present understanding of God.[37] Others, however, insist that a more far-reaching reconstruction of their religion's notions about God is needed. I have identified three main directions in which their search takes them: the incorporation of the feminine to the divine, liberation theology, and process thought.

Substantial historical work has been done by Phyllis Trible, a biblical scholar, and Eleanor McLaughlin, a historian, on the Feminine in God. They have exposed the various ways in which the Christian tradition has already incorporated and embraced an understanding of a feminine aspect of its image of God.[38] They assert that in the mainstream of Christian theology God is not an exclusively masculine entity, but denotes a deity who is neither male nor female. In manifestation to us, however, God is known through both male and female imagery.

Other Christian theorists see the need to incorporate this feminine imagery into the Christian understanding of God in a systematic and comprehensive way. Joan Chamberlain Engelsman explores the historical roots of the feminine imagery in the divine in Christianity, and various possibilities for reincorporating that feminine side of God. Based on an acceptance of the general psychoanalytic theory of repression, and a Jungian analysis of the archetypes, she accepts a feminine archetype as necessary for imaging the divine. This archetype was present in the past. It has been repressed, thereby producing much harm in Christianity. It needs to be reintegrated into the Christian tradition.

She argues that specific areas of Christian systematic theology need to be reformulated in order to reincorporate the repressed archetype: the doctrine of the Trinity, and the topic of the nature and origin of evil. She suggests three possibilities for reintroducing the feminine into the image of the divine: the description of one of the members of the Trinity as feminine; the development of the feminine aspect of all three members of the Trinity; or the addition of a female member to the Trinity and the formation of a quaternity. She does not, however, defend one of these options as preferable. She also assumes that because the feminine is deeply linked with evil and the dark side of the person, recognition of the feminine in God means the inclusion of evil in the image of the divine, who is not "predicted or confined by human standards of morality."[39]

Regrettably, Engelsman does not always make her assumptions clear. For instance, she holds much in common with Goldenberg. Although she wishes to retain much of the Christian religious system, her basis for religious decision-making seems to be as Jungian as it is Christian. Specifically, she is concerned with the function of religion in the psychic life of persons, and she decides the good or harm of keeping certain aspects of Christian tradition on the grounds of her Jungian model of psychic health. For Engelsman Jungian psychology is normative with respect to religion.

Some Christian feminists have found the contemporary theologies of liberation emergent from Third World culture to be most helpful in formulating a theological statement which expresses women's experience in the world and with the Christian tradition. From differing perspectives, Rosemary Radford Ruether and Letty M. Russell have produced the most thorough of the feminist liberation theologies. Ruether is not primarily concerned with writing about God, but about ethics. Consequently she seldom writes directly about God, but focuses on the concept of God as it affects human behavior in the process of the human movement toward liberation. Her primary concern is not with theology but with Christianity as a system, its corporate existence as a part of the world. Her Marxist analysis of society provides the major framework for her ethical critique of contemporary societies. She seeks to find "what transformations need to take place to transform Christianity from a Constantinian to a prophetic religion. . . ." The aim she states at the beginning of her *Liberation Theology* applies to much of her work: to "ask questions of the resources of the Christian tradition to provide symbols for the liberation of peoples whom the very culture created in the name of Christianity has helped to oppress."[40]

God must be understood primarily as the one who is the source of the world, who made it to live in ecological and social harmony, in a just and free society. The biblical version contains a "holistic view of creation and its future promise of redemption."[41] Christ is the presence of God's liberating power among human beings to move them to accept this mission of liberation for other persons and the world, which shares in human oppression. Ruether's work focuses on the prophetic mission of the church as agent of the message of freedom.

Russell develops her notion of God within the perspective of liberation theology much more extensively than Ruether. Her theology is overtly biblically based, and she explores various aspects of God which contribute to a more complete understanding of human liberation.

In her work on human liberation Russell insists that this human liberation is only properly rooted in a sense of the divine transcendence—divine freedom. A God who is bound by the world or identified with it cannot communicate the strength and grace that finite, sinful creatures need if they are to break their idols of God and of repressive socioeconomic structures. In recovering the various biblical names of God, we discover how we have limited our understanding of the divine freedom which could liberate us. We have also failed to appreciate the mutuality and the servant character of the divine relation to humanity.

Russell suggests that in a more thorough and complete biblical apprehension of God, we would focus on the way the persons of the Trinity transcend all human characteristics, but also include all types of human ways of being. The central metaphor of the relationship among persons of the Trinity is love, which is the internal life of God, which God as Creator, Liberator, and Comforter shares with creatures.[42]

In *The Future of Partnership*, Russell explores this fundamental apprehension of God in light of her basic metaphor for human interaction, partnership. The divine represents itself to us in connection with our personhood and identity, in our own discovery of our identity as partners with God through divine intervention. God is both Lord and servant, as we see if we follow biblical history, and this character can "aid us in the difficult process of overcoming our own dualistic hierarchies that so often undermine the possibility of partnership."[43] God as Lord and servant reveals two aspects of humanity when it acts as God's redeemed creation. First, the context of service is partnership, for true service of others can only be done within a context of a relationship of mutual love and respect, not in a situation in which one person is subordinate to the other. Second, the context of partnership is service. Just as God serves us so that our relationship of friendship with God can grow so also we serve others so that our partnership with them can be strengthened.[44]

Russell's liberation theology leads her to focus on those aspects of God that speak of the already and the not-yet character of the reign of God. She is not too concerned with the psychological aspects of the biblical imagery, but with the theme of God the liberator in a social, political, and religious context. Russell's theology is biblically centered and she assumes a fundamental loyalty to the biblical tradition as the norm for her thought.

Other feminist theologians write of God in ways that combine certain interpretations of process thought with liberation theology. Although she is still developing her own theological approach, Carter Heyward has been very well received in the Christian feminist community. In a loose sense, one might call her a pantheist, because she describes God primarily as the power of relation known in the world. In "In the Beginning Is the Relation: Toward a Christian Ethic of Sexuality," Heyward notes that Jesus, the crucified and risen Lord, is not the center of Christian consciousness. Rather, God is the center, and "God is at the center of human life *in* human form and activity." Her theological conclusion is that "in praxis—in both our activity and our reflection upon what we do—*humanity* stands at the center for those who profess to be followers of Jesus."[45] In ethics and in her understanding of God, relationship is primary. "That which is most ultimate, most valuable, [is] Relationality, Co-creativity."[46]

Heyward understands relationship to encompass not only one-to-one interactions, but also a wide range of social interrelationships, including national and international. Thus concerns in the cause of justice and power are essential parts of her ethics, as well as sexuality and more individualized issues, because all are valuable aspects of the creation. However, the quality of relationship among humans is the ultimate value. Heyward regards God as the power who animates relationship. In building the future, she suggests we will be "empowered by God, who is nothing other than the power of love in history, the power for right-relation in history, the power of justice in the world."[47]

Although she has not yet systematized the interaction between themes of process theology and liberation theology, Heyward uses ideas from both to express a fundamentally pantheistic vision in which God moves humans toward a community in which each is valued and all are interdependent. Heyward focuses primarily on the human, rather than on the cosmos. This focus sets her off from most process thinkers. Her use of the notion of relation, so central to her thought, is certainly in accord with process thought, as is her focus on the interrelatedness of all that is. Her ethics reflect her concern with liberation theology and the search for justice in the movement of the human community.

Carol Ochs asserts a strongly pantheistic position from a theological base. She understands the classical Christian tradition as having represented God as spiritual, transcendent, perfect, and infinite, and the world as the opposite. She suggests, however, "that God is not apart from, separate from, or other than this reality. We, all together, are part of the Whole, the All in All . . . not other than, distinct from, or opposed to creation."[48] Eternity and transcendence can be understood as perspectives. For instance, eternity is the sense of the relationship of any individual person or event to the Whole. The Whole is transcendent in the sense that it is greater than any individual part, but it is not different from the sum of its parts, the world which we see and know.

Ochs's monism or pantheism represents a very explicit attempt to cut through all the debate about God and Goddess, and solve the problem by denying any personal or conscious reality to divinity. God or the divine is the name for the whole of the world of visible experience. For the feminist this permits the elimination of an oppressive structure of religion, which has used God to perpetuate a false view of the world and human relations in it.

One should also note that for both Heyward and Ochs, an important aspect of their understanding of God is its positive valuation of the physical. In common with many other feminists, they regard the abolition of the dualism between spirit and matter as essential to a genuinely human vision of the world. Thus for them the concept of God must include matter, feeling, mind. God is therefore necessarily the whole which we experience. For Heyward this whole is represented primarily as human centered; Ochs would focus more on the cosmos.

Christ and the Revelation of God

If the figure of God is rejected by some feminists, Jesus Christ is repudiated even more absolutely. Naomi Goldenberg rejects Jesus Christ totally because he is the male embodiment of the divinity. Therefore, simply because of who he is, he contributes to the suppression of women and their sense of psychic inferiority.[49]

Mary Daly also rejects the Christ. Practically, she notes that the maleness of Jesus has been used by clergy as an excuse to suppress women. In addition, the particularity of the Incarnation in the person of Jesus obscures the power of the "New Being" in all human beings. Daly argues that in a patriarchal religion the clearest bearers of the "New Being" should be the aliens, such as women, rather than a representative of the class of oppressive males.

Particularly offensive for Daly is the figure of Jesus as the sacrificial victim. Often Christians put the blame for Jesus' death on others, laying blame for their own wrongdoing on others. The woman's role as scapegoat has been encouraged by Christianity, especially in connection with the myth of the fall and feminine evil. Not only are the negative qualities of a victim projected on women, but the sacrificial qualities idealized by Christianity in Christ are particularly nurtured in women. But because the original guilt for evil is projected on them, women can never be innocent victims like Jesus, and thus gain neither credit for sacrifice nor the dignity of an active role.[50] Consequently, the Christ-figure is used to oppress women in ways they cannot escape.

Daly argues that none of the theological responses to these objections takes seriously the significance of the Christ-figure in the actual oppression of women. Even the use of the symbol of Mary has been used to oppress women, rather than to liberate them.[51]

In studying Daly's objections to Jesus Christ one is not surprised that there is no mention of Christ in *Gyn/Ecology*. Daly's argument is closed. Marjorie Suchocki, in an analysis of Daly's position, argues that the male savior represents the "repudiation of women," which is the source of the suppression of women.[52] Daly, most emphatically of all the radical feminist theorists, asserts the absolute incompatibility of "this fixation on Jesus"[53] and any true feminism.

In Christian feminist circles there has been remarkably little direct response to Daly and Goldenberg's explicit and uncompromising challenge. Suchocki, in her article about Daly's attack on Christology, acknowledges that in fact the image of Christ in popular Christian tradition has contributed to the continued oppression of women in reducing them to dependence and submission. Suchocki counters that feminists have experienced in Christ a liberating vision of which he is the source, but at the same time they are challenged by Daly to "reconsider Christology, writing if possible a Christology which is neither sexist nor exploitable in sexist agendas."[54]

Concurring with Daly's assessment of the oppressive character of patriarchal religion, Suchocki also argues that many women have been liberated within this religion to live lives of achievement and happiness. Their energy is better honored, Suchocki contends, if we acknowledge that patriarchal religion needs to be transformed through being respun, rewoven.[55] By eliminating the dualism and male dominance in Christianity, feminists may revitalize Christianity through their own experience, their women-energy.[56] She does not predict the outcome, but proclaims the hope and possibility of making the transformation.

Rita Brock has essayed a more systematic approach to a reconstruction of Christology from a feminist perspective. She identifies the basic question about Christology as being soteriological: from what are we redeemed? In what sense is Christ a *savior*?[57] If sin is not being God-centered, as Augustine of Hippo claimed, what does woman's experience say to that issue? Instead of answering that question directly Brock identifies characteristics of Jesus' humanity relevant to the question: his sense of call from God, his worldly powerlessness, preaching and creating of community, and death at the hands of the powerful because of his confrontation with them.[58]

She asserts that "the Christian tradition has tended to see the Christ event as the one incarnational act of a transcendent God." But if that dualism is rejected, we can reconstruct the questions of Christology to ask ourselves how we can stand where Jesus did, and walk our journeys "with his presence as somehow resonant with our own centers." We can also inquire about the way Jesus reveals to us the presence of God among us.[59] From the perspective of process thought,[60] Christology itself becomes a way of expressing the unity of body-spirit, self-others, and persons-world. The resurrection is God's way of proclaiming the "renewing power of God and the earth to bear."[61] Jesus connects several redemptive insights: that deity comes to us embodied, that God is "relational, gracious, and forgiving, and that God calls us to be interdependent."[62] God offers us in Christ freedom and wholeness, a vision which is diametrically opposed to patriarchal oppression.

Burton Cooper, in "Metaphysics, Christology, and Sexism," tries to indicate ways in which process theology offers a way to overcome two lines of attack made on the doctrine of the Incarnation. The first comes from some contemporary English theologians in *The Myth of God Incarnate,* and the second from Mary Daly.[63] Cooper rejects certain theologians' efforts to respond to Daly's criticisms by explaining Jesus' maleness as part of the scandal of particularity. He suggests that process Christology offers the best response to Daly's objections because it removes "any metaphysical grounds for the appropriation of male language into trinitarian dogma."[64]

Rather than speaking of a metaphysical union in the incarnation, one must speak of "an existential, 'prehensive' communion." By this Cooper means that Jesus' life is a "struggle towards communion." Jesus responded to God in such a way that he felt the world as God did and responded according to God's intention even when he was not certain of what that meant. Jesus' sexuality is not ontologically significant. Cooper suggests that such a process Christology will both "abort" sexism in Christology and "give birth, in due time, to a strengthened incarnational faith."[65]

Joan Chamberlain Engelsman argues that in late biblical Judaism and the intertestamental period, the doctrine of *Sophia* was extremely important. In Hellenistic Judaism the feminine figure of Sophia, Wisdom, was replaced by the masculine Logos. In Judaism she was relegated to a minor place in heaven and in Christianity her attributes were all transferred to Christ. As a result of this transference, Engelsman notes, all direct access to the feminine dimension of God was lost in Christianity.[66] Because of theological developments, presumably in Christology, Engelsman does not suggest Sophiology as the source for the reexpression of the feminine in the divine. Among several possibilities for the reintroduction of the feminine in the image of the divine, she suggests but does not develop the notion that the feminine aspects of all three persons of the Trinity might be developed. She finds precedence for this in Clement of Alexandria and the Odes of Solomon.[67]

The most comprehensive theological treatment of the issue is by Letty Russell, who from a liberation theology perspective explores both the doctrine of the Trinity and the meaning of the person of Christ for all human beings. She uses the classical categories of the economic and the immanent Trinity to distinguish between God's "dynamic communication of love between the persons of the Trinity."[68] She perceives the Trinity as representing the partnership of God within the divine reality and with human beings. On the basis of this conception of partnership, she outlines the role of God with people in the world as "caring for creation, setting the captives free, and standing as witnesses for and with those who need an advocate."[69]

For us humans Christ is the representative of this trinitarian God—creator, liberator, and advocate. Russell takes very seriously the notion of Christ as the representative of God; because he is the representative of God he is the one who is able to liberate humanity, exemplifying the divine acceptance of all and the inclusion of even the most oppressed in the divine kingdom.[70] The salvation that Jesus brings is interpreted by Russell as the message of liberation from the bonds of dualisms that divide and earthly bondage of a political, social, and personal sort.[71]

Not only is Christ the representative to us of the trinitarian God, he is also the representative of the new humanity, he is the Prince of Shalom. Because he manifests to us our togetherness, our partnership with God, he shows us what it is to be human as God's children. In Christ the forgiveness of our sins is given as is our openness to the future with God. At the center of the life of Christ is the cross, showing God's suffering through Christ's humanity with us, calling us to identify ourselves with the one who suffers for others. Through faith women and men can participate with Christ in showing the new humanity, liberated and together with God and others.[72]

Two titles used of Jesus in the New Testament best sum up the liberating aspect of his work: he is Lord and Servant. He is acclaimed by the disciples as Lord, and known as the Suffering Servant. This apparent contradiction underlines the unique aspect of Jesus' representation of the divine: "The meaning of God's Lordship in Jesus Christ is clear only in relation to the purpose of that Lordship, which is service. The purpose of God's service and subordination in Jesus Christ is to establish the Lordship of God's Love."[73] As Lord of love, who serves others, Christ shows us the basis for genuine partnership, in which we are partners with God in liberating the world, but also partners with each other, overcoming the bonds of race, sex, class.[74]

Rosemary Radford Ruether explores the relationship between belief in Christ and several cultural issues, including feminism, in *To Change the World*.[75] She outlines the contemporary debate and isolates the fundamental question: is Christology so bound up with the oppressive structures of patriarchy that it has any redemptive value for women?[76]

She identifies three models of Christology that are present in the Christian tradition in order to ask whether or not they have redemptive possibilities for women: the imperial Christ, who unites Hebrew messianism and Greek Logos philosophy; androgynous Christologies, such as Julian of Norwich's mother Jesus or the Shakers' dual Christ; and prophetic iconoclastic relationships, which respond authentically to other human beings and point us to the new humanity.[77]

Ruether does not see any of these models as valueless for feminism, remarking that the imperial Christ could be developed in more positive directions and that the androgynous Christ points up the inadequacy of a purely male identification of Christ for the redemption of all humanity. She appears, however, to prefer the third alternative. In all her writings the Christ of liberation theology has been the most helpful christological model. It focuses on the meaning of Christ in the transformation of social conditions and the renewal of the whole of humanity in the light of divine justice.

RESPONSES TO THE DIFFERING
APPROACHES

Again, we have observed a wide range of opinions expressed by feminists. Although some common concerns are woven through all these points of view, significant differences are articulated among the various theorists and cannot always be harmonized. This is true even in the case of opinions about the term used to designate the divine reality.

Should one speak of the Goddess or God? One cannot even continue the discussion without some answer for oneself. In the most profound sense, I suggest that this is the wrong question to be focusing on, because in the Christian Scriptures there is no generalized "God," but a specific named deity who is the object of worship. In the Hebrew Bible one addresses the Holy One, Yahweh, Elohim, the Lord, the Most High, and so forth. In the New Testament one worships the one who is in heaven, the God and the Father of our Lord Jesus Christ, the Holy Spirit, and the Word who existed from the beginning and came to dwell among us.[78] Worship is rendered by the Christian to the God-Father, the Word-Son, and the Holy Spirit in whose name the Christian is baptized and enters into relationship. Among the attributes given to the divine reality are included many feminine characteristics and even feminine names. Consequently, to pose the question as to "God" or "Goddess" is to run the risk of ignoring the complexity of the biblical understanding of the divine reality worshiped and does not adequately take into account the inclusiveness of the image of the biblical deity. Whether the riches of the biblical tradition have been sufficiently appreciated is certainly questionable, but the riches are surely there to be appropriated.

I have chosen to use the term God as a general designation, representing the functional aspect of the divine as the one worthy of worship, rather than using it as a personal designation. I have so chosen for two reasons. The first is that "Goddess" calls attention to femaleness rather than to function, as do the words "poetess" or "songstress." Such female endings are commonly used to imply inferiority (female diminutive = inferior). Although it might be possible to argue that such a female word might be used as a badge of honor, I have chosen the term which most clearly for most readers designates the divine as object of worship, without explicit gender designation. In addition, because the biblical notions of the deity encompass masculine and feminine characteristics and language, I have kept the term God on the grounds that the term for the biblical deity can itself be quite useful; the issue is how to help people appropriate the various biblical images.

The second reason relates to the word *God* as representative of a function rather than a personal designation. The *Oxford English Dictionary* traces the fascinating origin of the term, noting that its proper parallel in Latin is *numen* rather than *deus*. A significant element of the Christian tradition chooses to emphasize that the divine reality is suprapersonal, not personal in the sense of our psychologically oriented, gender-specific identifications. Thus I have chosen to retain the term *God* in its most basic sense. Although I recognize the dangers, I have chosen to keep the traditional Christian term, using it in its most fundamental sense.

Beyond questions about using the term God, significant conflict emerges from the very issue of what is meant by the divine reality. Mary Daly increasingly moves away from her notion of God the Verb, not advocating any notion of the divine; Naomi Goldenberg rejects any deity except as a tool for psychological development of women, who need a more positive self-image. Some advocate the Goddess as a life power in the world to which women are particularly attuned, others refuse to be so circumscribed.

Among those who speak of God, every view from monism to liberation theology prevails. Of the major theological writers, only Letty Russell is concerned to develop an explicitly biblical theology. She is also the only one who attempts to relate the Christian understanding of the Trinity to feminism by focusing on the inclusiveness and non-gender-specific nature of the Trinity.

Despite these very real and wide divergences in their understanding of God, these Christian feminists *and* the radical feminists do share in a search for the wholeness of the human community with all that is. From Goldenberg, who stresses the psychological health of women and their need to find their own internal wholeness as well as that with the world, to Russell, who seeks to explore liberation within the context of the relationship of the whole cosmos to God, all are seeking to express the fundamental interrelatedness of all that is. A person's acceptance of any perspective depends on how well the individual concerned believes that a particular viewpoint permits human integrity and a full interrelationship of the various aspects of the self with the world.

But if one may trace those common threads in the responses to the notion of the divine, a major difference emerges when we look at the issue of Christ. A perusal, for instance, of Mary Daly's rejection of Christ, especially because of the sacrificial nature of Christ's life and death, alongside Letty Russell's affirmation of the servanthood and sacrificial death of Christ would seem to leave no grounds for reconciliation. Christ's maleness poses an insuperable barrier for Daly, but for Christian feminists that is not the case, either because they in one way or another do not accept the incarnation of Christ as unique in its classical sense, or because they see God revealed in Christ in ways that very explicitly overcome the male/female division.

In this book I will try to respond to the insights of various feminist thinkers under three rubrics: what is the human, who is the Christ, and what is meant by God. In my efforts I hope to weave into this response various values of feminism together with fidelity to the Christian tradition.

NOTES

1. Mary Daly, *Beyond God the Father: Towards a Philosophy of Women's Liberation* (Boston: Beacon Press, 1973), 8.

2. Ibid., 15.

3. Mary Daly, *Gyn/Ecology* (Boston: Beacon Press, 1978), xii.

4. Ibid., 39–42, 319–20, 354–424.

5. Carol P. Christ, *Diving Deep and Surfacing: Women Writers on Spiritual Quest* (Boston: Beacon Press, 1980), xi.

6. Ibid., 119–20.

7. Ibid., 126–31.

8. Penelope Washbourn, *Becoming Woman: The Quest for Wholeness in Female Experience* (New York: Harper & Row, 1975), xiv.

9. Ann Belford Ulanov, *Receiving Woman: Studies in the Psychology and Theology of the Feminine* (Philadelphia: Westminster Press, 1981), 18.

10. Ibid., 26.

11. Ibid., 146–47.

12. Ibid., 158–63.

13. Ibid., 167–69, 173–74.

14. Carol Heilbrun, *Reinventing Womanhood* (New York: W.W. Norton & Co., 1979), 95.

15. Ibid., 208–11.

16. Letty M. Russell, *Human Liberation in a Feminist Perspective* (Philadelphia: Westminster Press, 1974), 63–65.

17. Ibid., 145–54.

18. Letty M. Russell, *The Future of Partnership* (Philadelphia: Westminster Press, 1979), 46–53.

19. Christ, *Diving Deep and Surfacing*, 119–31.

20. Rosemary Radford Ruether, "Liberation and Countercultural Feminism," *Christian Century* 97 (10 September 1980): 844–45.

21. Gilbert Russell and Margaret Dewey, "Psychological Aspects," in *Man, Woman, Priesthood*, ed. Peter Moore (London: SPCK, 1978), 95.

22. Carol Christ, "Why Women Need the Goddess," in *Womanspirit Rising*, ed. Carol Christ and Judith Plaskow (New York: Harper & Row, 1979), 278.

23. Patricia Wilson-Kastner, "Christianity and New Feminist Religions," *Christian Century* 98 (9 September 1981): 864–68.

24. Naomi Goldenberg, *The Changing of the Gods* (Boston: Beacon Press, 1973), 3.

25. Ibid., 32–36.

26. Ibid., 47.

27. Ibid., 89.

28. Carol Christ, "Why Women Need the Goddess," in *Womanspirit Rising*, 273–88.

29. Christ, *Diving Deep and Surfacing*, 128.

30. *Womanspirit Rising*, 278–79.

31. Starhawk, *The Spiral Dance* (New York: Harper & Row, 1979), 7.

32. Ibid., 9.

33. Ibid., 14–15, 77–78.

34. Ibid., 81.

35. Daly, *Beyond God the Father*, 90–97, 198.

36. Daly, *Gyn/Ecology*, 111.

37. E.g., Georgia Harkness, in *Women in Church and Society* (Nashville: Abingdon Press, 1972), advocates the equality of women in the church, writes of this change as a revolution, reassesses the status of women in the Bible to point up this equality, but never mentions the notion of God and Christ as concepts which need to be reexamined from a feminist perspective (pp. 26–71).

38. E.g., Phyllis Trible, *God and the Rhetoric of Sexuality*, Overtures to Biblical Scholarship (Philadelphia: Fortess Press, 1978); Eleanor McLaughlin, "The Christian Past: Does It Hold a Future for Women?" in *Womanspirit Rising*, 93–105; Leonard Swidler's *Biblical Affirmations of Women* (Philadelphia: Westminster Press, 1979) contains much material used by feminists.

39. Joan Chamberlain Engelsman, *The Feminine Dimension of the Divine* (Philadelphia: Westminster Press, 1979), 155.

40. Rosemary Radford Ruether, *Liberation Theology: Human Hope Confronts Christian History and American Power* (New York: Paulist Press, 1972), 1.

41. Ibid., 8.

42. Russell, *Human Liberation,* 101–103.

43. Russell, *Future of Partnership,* 67.

44. Ibid., 73–77.

45. Carter Heyward, "In the Beginning Is the Relation: Towards a Christian Ethic of Sexuality," *Integrity Forum* 7 (Lent 1981): 2; her doctoral dissertation, now published as *The Redemption of God: A Theology of Mutual Relation* (Washington, D.C.: Univ. Press of America, 1982) elaborates these themes.

46. Heyward, "In the Beginning Is the Relation," 6.

47. Ibid.

48. Carol Ochs, *Behind the Sex of God* (Boston: Beacon Press, 1977).

49. Goldenberg, *Changing of the Gods.*

50. Daly, *Beyond God the Father,* 69–77.

51. Ibid., 77–90.

52. Marjorie Suchocki, "The Challenge of Mary Daly," *Encounter* 41 (1980): 310.

53. Daly, *Beyond God the Father,* 70.

54. Suchocki, "Challenge of Mary Daly," 312.

55. Ibid., 314.

56. Ibid., 315.

57. Rita Brock, "A Feminist Consciousness Looks at Christology," *Encounter* 41 (1980): 321.

58. Ibid., 324–25.

59. Ibid.

60. Lewis Ford, in *The Lure of God* (Philadelphia: Fortress Press, 1978), 45–70, provides a helpful brief overview of recent process Christology.

61. Rita Brock, "Feminist Consciousness Looks at Christology," 326.

62. Ibid., 329.

63. Burton Cooper, "Metaphysics, Christology, and Sexism: An Essay in Philosophical Theology," *Religious Studies* 16 (June 1980): 179–93.

64. Ibid., 193.

65. Ibid.

66. Engelsman, *Feminine Dimension of the Divine,* 74–120.

67. Ibid., 152–53.

68. Russell, *Future of Partnership,* 29.

69. Ibid., 34–35.

70. Ibid., 61 (cf. Russell, *Human Liberation,* 87).

71. Ibid., 111.

72. Ibid., 135–40.

73. Russell, *Future of Partnership,* 62–67 (cf. *Human Liberation,* 140–42).

74. Ibid., 152–54.

75. Rosemary Radford Ruether, *To Change the World: Christology and Cultural Criticism* (New York: Crossroad, 1981).

76. Ibid., 47.

77. Ibid., 48–56.

78. Useful introductions to the conventional wisdom about the complexity of the biblical notion of "God" may be found in the *Interpreter's Dictionary of the Bible,* 2: 407–36. A more detailed study of the feminine dimensions of this notion may be found in Trible's *God and the Rhetoric of Sexuality.* See also Swidler, *Biblical Affirmations of Women,* esp. 21–73; Raphael Patai, *The Hebrew Goddess* (New York: Avon Books, 1967); and James Edgar Burns, *God as Woman, Woman as God* (New York: Paulist Press, 1973). Karl Rahner (in "Theos in the New Testament," in *Theological Investigations* [Baltimore: Helicon Press, 1961], 1: 79–148) also explores the complexity of the New Testament usage of the term "God."

CHAPTER 2

Another Way of
Looking at the World

STARTING WITH HUMAN KNOWING

Why begin by discussing the way in which human beings know? If we are seeking to salvage, renew, or reconstruct Christology, why not proceed to Christology proper rather than dawdle with extraneous questions? We must raise clear questions as we endeavor to seek renewal in our theology. In his monumental work, *Insight: A Study of Human Understanding,* Bernard Lonergan articulated the grounds for such a search: "Thoroughly understand what it is to understand, and not only will you understand the broad lines of all there is to be understood, but you will also possess a fixed base, an invariant pattern, opening upon all further developments of understanding."[1]

I do not pretend to be sketching a completely new epistemology here. As we have seen, however, feminism has questioned modern Western ways of thinking and knowing, and our perceptions of reality.

Several factors impel me to present my own responses to these questions in an attempt to develop a feminist theology. Although I have noted certain fundamental shared concerns and values among feminists, it is equally clear that there are some basic contradictions about significant matters which make it impossible to discern one comprehensive feminist theory of knowing. Some of these issues are obvious from the beginning; others are not. For instance, some claim that men and women "know" in fundamentally different ways. Others say that we may speak of various ways of human knowing, with various cultural, biological, psychic, and other factors impinging on it. One might ask about subdivisions in the categories of knowing: Does a feminist male know differently from one who is not? Does a woman who accepts and profits from her oppressed status know in the same way as a feminist? One could continue this line of inquiry, but I think that these questions reflect the inadequacy of present theories and make it difficult simply to accept one of the present feminist theories.

I am not going to try to refute various feminists or to immerse myself into the one correct approach, an adversarial male game which strikes me as being inappropriate for theology. Theology, I believe, ought to persuade through intrinsic appeal of the presentation. I will attempt to outline the main lines of a theological exploration of human knowing which, so it seems to me, is respectful of the insights of feminism and also coherent enough to provide an adequate base for exploring the theological questions that need to be addressed.

This enterprise is particularly important in a period which is open to considering various points of view. A post-Einstein age no longer permits us the luxury of assuming that there is one and only one way of understanding anything. Even the classic Aristotelian tradition recognized that the very same reality could be observed from a variety of points of view, and could therefore be described differently depending on the type of questions asked. In a generation of postcritical philosophy, non-Euclidian geometry, Freudian and post-Freudian psychology, and interplanetary exploration, in our twentieth-century culture, we are increasingly aware that both the subject and the object, as well as the perspective, are constantly changing. Thus we are indeed open to new and various epistemologies and aware that any theory of knowledge must take account of rapid and constant change in ourselves and the reality we are knowing.

In the context of contemporary openness to new approaches to the study of human knowing any feminist epistemology also must incorporate a sense that the dualistic, scientifically oriented analysis of knowing which has dominated the Western intellectual world for about the last five hundred years is in need of radical change, if not replacement. Some philosophers, such as Michael Polanyi, would retain a basic principle which has characterized modern Western philosophy: a confidence in the possibility of rational analysis. He also desires to add other dimensions: a concern for specifically personal, nonanalytic knowing which helps permit a more adequate grasp of the total act of knowing.[2] Others, like Vine Deloria, in *The Metaphysic of Modern Existence,* reject the whole development of Western philosophy and theology, and challenge it to adopt a more holistic, nonscientific, nonrationalistic approach.[3] My efforts will be more modest.

PERCEIVING THE WORLD

What I propose to do at this juncture is to outline the principles involved in a theory of knowing that would be in accord with the feminist concerns we have noted and would also aid us in articulating Christology anew. The first appropriate question for consideration would thus seem to be about the ways in which human beings perceive the world.

Without resorting to a technical analysis, the best way of describing human knowledge is that we perceive the world as a differentiated whole, that is, we physically perceive, intellectually understand, and emotionally relate to the world as a unity, or a whole, although we also apprehend parts of this whole. We intellectually understand those patterns which we cannot directly perceive, but which we infer from what we apprehend. Our very process of knowing presses us to seek for greater wholes, to make general statements out of particulars, to find coherence from the parts and pieces which are available to us. At different times and in different situations our knowing may focus on the differentiation and sometimes on the wholeness, but both are parts of the dynamic which seeks to understand the totality.[4]

At the root of this approach is the fundamental assumption that the human subject can know something about the world outside its own mind. In aiming toward the whole we are in some real way able to touch a physical-mental world which exists in its own integrity, and to know something about it. From the perspective of a feminist, the radical dissociation of the internal feeling, thinking self from the body and the "world out there," which was so forcefully expressed by René Descartes in the early seventeenth century and articulated so absolutely by Immanuel Kant in the late eighteenth century, is based on unacceptable assumptions. Just as the Kantian critique of epistemology was based on an assumption that the knowing subject was confined to itself and the contents of its consciousness, the feminist approach is based on an assumption that the knowing subject is a psychophysical reality which perceives the greater reality of which it is a part and is integrated into the greater reality it perceives. A critical philosophy can be built on the base of such an axiom, but assumes the fundamental link between the knower and the world of which she or he is a part.

The fundamental assertion that the knower is part of the whole she or he knows is crucial to feminist epistemology. Recently feminists and others have dealt with the ways in which male-dominated philosophy and science have discussed the way in which we know the world. Carolyn Merchant's incisive *The Death of Nature: Women, Ecology, and the Scientific Revolution* explores "the formation of a world view and a science that, by reconceptualizing reality as a machine rather than a living organism, sanctioned the domination of both nature and women."[5] Merchant focuses on the change in values in postmedieval science and philosophy which no longer presented humans as part of a living organic nature, but as people who could and should dominate and control nature. Because the philosophers and scientists were male, part of a dominant male hierarchy, both scientific attitudes toward nature and ideas about the status and role of women exuded prejudices and values of sexism. Both nature and women were "other," passive, and needed to be dominated and shaped according to the superior male plans. If males who truly and impartially perceived the world acted to divide, analyze, and reshape nature and women only then could the subordinate realities achieve their real, though limited, potential.

In a vision of knower and known as part of one whole, those values which are found in a divisive approach to the world are intolerable. A world-view based on a search for the whole also excludes another myth of the popular scientific world-view, that of objectivity and impassivity in scientific knowing. With deep-seated roots in the Greek philosophical disdain of emotions, a profound faith in the validity of quantitative measurement, and an assumption that the male investigator knew what ought to be done, philosophical and scientific enterprises never questioned their fundamental validity or the rightness of their actions and their questions.

I have treated modern Western philosophy and science together because they share the same Enlightenment rationality which attempts to know through pure reason, dissociated from other factors. Immanuel Kant and Isaac Newton exemplify the spirit of Enlightenment philosophy and science, which is a continuing influence on Western thought up to the present. I am aware that contemporary science is quite conscious of its own relativity and that of the knower and the known, as well as the various factors of emotion and nonrational intuition which are present in all human knowing, including scientific, but the attitudes remain in our popular technological culture.[6] Nonquantifiable, nonanalyzable, or nonverifiable elements were assumed to be invalid or irrelevant. Women particularly were to be either patronized or despised because they embodied those uncontrollable emotions which were the opposite of true science and analytic philosophy.

But today scientists and philosophers alike recognize with increasing frequency that emotions, nonverifiable assumptions, and suprarational values undergird and are suffused throughout so-called scientific systems. All scientific and philosophical systems, for instance, are based on a nonrational commitment which assumes that the quest for any sort of knowledge is possible and worthwhile, and that the search for truth is worth living for. One may assume certain sorts of questions to be better than other sorts, but the reasons why one might want to ask those sorts of questions at all are neither rational nor provable. Such assertions do not invalidate scientific endeavors, but they do point out both the partial and incomplete character of the nature of the questions asked, and the nonrational basis on which such a supposedly completely rational activity is founded. A feminist epistemology seeks to find ways to integrate the affective as well as the rational, and to show the total personal foundations of the process of knowing.

The activity of knowing is a process of growth, not simply one act or a discrete series of acts. Human knowing is cumulative, as one would expect in a description of the way in which human beings relate themselves to the whole of which they are a part. Because beings exist temporally and physically, their interrelationships are extended in time and space, and human mental activity must extend in time and space also, with the capacity to grasp complex temporal and spatial interconnections. To understand knowing as a process means identifying the components and understanding their relationship, as well as the way in which the actual process of growth takes place.

In the act of knowing, the subject, the "I" and the rest of the world, including other "I's," as well as conscious and nonconscious beings, are related to each other in the consciousness of the subject. A knower is one who relates all these elements to each other, not simply as pieces side by side, but as parts of a whole. The process is fraught with tension, because in knowing, nothing stays still. Everything is in constant interaction, always changing, always moving. As in a kaleidoscope, all the elements are modified as their relationship to each other alters and shifts, and constantly new appearances emerge as pieces move.

Knowing is not simply mental awareness of random occurrences, however. To know is to assemble the pieces into a pattern, and to see how the patterns relate to each other, as well as to distinguish one part of the pattern from another so that one may understand the interrelation of the parts of the pattern to its whole. Each insight, each vision, relates to another, and the person constantly aims toward a more complex vision of the whole by exploring the various patterns and creating more and more complex wholes. One may measure growth in understanding at least in part through the increasing facility an individual subject shows in her or his ability to differentiate the various parts while being able to understand increasingly complex wholes, and the relationship of each part to the whole. The maturing knower has strong ego-boundaries and appreciates the limits of others, while at the same time retaining a strong sense of the connections of one to the other.

The dynamic of this knowing process expresses itself in human memory and expectation. One's present perceptions and hopes and fears for the future are rooted in the way in which one has remembered and integrated one's past perceptions. Reality can "make sense" only if the human person is animated in the wellspring of her or his conscious life by the urge to know the whole, and the mental equipment to constantly put all the events and perceptions of the whole into the perspective of totality the person seeks. To remember the past is to recall it so that it is a lively whole, composed of a variety of events. By and large, one remembers those events, and even mentally distorts them, so that they do contribute to the comprehensible world-view one is seeking. Within the human mind is a dynamic that seeks understanding of the whole of reality, not just bits and pieces.

When one speculates about the future one is not simply spinning tales out of nothing; even the most outrageous science fiction bases itself on those perceptions of reality we already have, and creates versions of a whole we wish or fear. Various visions of the future, as well as more inchoate hopes and fears, all depend on our increasing awareness of what the totality of the world is, and what it is becoming.

At the same time one speaks of the dynamic changes of the knowing process, one has to remember that the knower and the known are also changing. Classical epistemology well appreciated that one could appropriately consider the same reality from several different perspectives; today there is an increasing appreciation that the knower also is constantly growing, acting and being acted upon, capable of apprehending and understanding more, able to compare, criticize, to make increasingly complex interrelationships. The whole internal affective-cognitive life of the knower is changing, as are the lives of other subjects with whom the "I" is a part of the world. All of the interrelationships and interactions of these beings are in constant flux.

Consequently, when one thinks about the whole which human beings are trying to know, one can no longer speak of static entities which are presently complete, because both individuals and the complex whole of all individuals together are changing at each moment. Thus when one refers to the "whole," one refers to two related but distinct notions. The whole signifies a reality present here and now in the complex interrelationship of all the various beings of the cosmos, and yet the same term, the whole, also signifies a direction in which the cosmos is developing.

The most suitable metaphor for the whole is that of an organism, a living being, with various parts which exist together to make a whole, yet which is changing to become something which it both is and is not yet. Like a person maturing, the whole grows and develops according to its own internal dynamic. Its changes are not random, but have their own integrity, intelligibility, and intentionality. Once one makes the act of faith and love in the process of knowing, the most coherent outcome is the affirmation of the whole as that which one is coming to know, that of which one is a part, and that toward which all is becoming.[7]

INTEGRATING THE WHOLE

Certain characteristics of knowing and the knower can be drawn from the model of the knowing process which I have outlined. They are not the only possible ones, but they seem to me to be significant for a fuller understanding of the self and the relation of the self to the whole, and will be part of later discussion about Christology.

The "I" who knows is a psychophysical unity. By that phrase I mean simply that an individual is a complex of physical being in the world and also that certain activities which depend on the physical nonetheless cannot be simply reduced to them. Even if, for instance, stimulation of a particular part of the brain produces a particular response, that response cannot simply be reduced to the physical, but involves expression in feeling and words, and usually varies from individual to individual. Furthermore, human beings are self-conscious and self-reflective, and the unique complexities of each individual do not seem susceptible to any clear or certain psychological or philosophical analysis.

Ever since the work of Aristotle, philosophers and theorists have recognized this unique interrelationship in the human person, but even as people have tried to explain the interaction between the physical and psychic aspects of the person, no one really seems to have found a complete answer. I have no intention of trying to match wits with such thinkers as Aristotle, Descartes, and Gilbert Ryle. Instead, I would merely suggest that a recognition of human existence as a unity with interconnected physical-spiritual, cognitive-affective dimensions would seem to me to be axiomatic for any attempt to understand or express the whole of human experience.

We human beings experience other selves and the world about through the body, through which we hear, see, become acquainted with others, interact with them, and encounter ourselves. The mind is utterly dependent on the body for that which it knows, feels, apprehends, touches, loves, and hates. Yet at the same time that the physical is always the beginning of knowledge, it is never the end. The act of knowing itself, even the simplest act of perception, is not simply physical. Rather, the mind takes, shapes, reacts, and integrates even the most insignificant physical experience. The more complex the mental activity, the more shaping, responding, and integrating of the world must be done by the cognitive-affective dimension of the human person called spirit.[8] The impetus of the spiritual dimension of the human person is to try to both understand and feel one's experience as part of a more meaningful, more complete whole.

Thomas Aquinas and Bernard Lonergan speak of this drive as the human search for intelligibility; others, such as Augustine or Henri Bergson, would express this desire more as an orientation of the whole person to will and be at one with the totality of that which is. Some would express this as God, others as a more immanent life force. For the moment the important point is that all human knowing contains an element of search for both belonging and transcendence. The knower seeks to incorporate x and y into a greater and more meaningful whole; the great human desire is not only to "see how it all fits together," but to experience belonging to a greater whole. Even those most isolated from experience in mental illness fantasize worlds in which they belong. They are not fleeing from wholeness, but creating a whole which they feel will not reject them.

One may thus perceive a dynamic of immanence/transcendence in the very process of human knowing and relating to the world. The very nature of the human relation to the whole involves an ever-active process of physical perception and critical psychic integration of that sensation. The person perceives and reacts affectively as well as intellectually, and both emotion and thought become and are made part of a greater whole. The more aware the person is, emotionally or cognitively, the more the person seeks the whole, being attracted to truth and beauty. The more the person transcends the particular to direct it to the whole, the more the individual is attuned to the significance of the particular, the moment, the specific, and is also able to relate it to a growing comprehension of the whole.

Although it is an obvious aspect of human knowing, it will perhaps not be wasteful to emphasize that all human knowing is relational. The "I" is only potential until it is awakened by the other; the other must be perceived and received by the "I" in order to be known. Knowing and being known are relationships, albeit of many possible different kinds and qualities, from intense close personal friendship to knowledge of an algebraic formula. In any case of knowing, both the knower and the known are different. The whole of reality is also modified by these relationships, as they develop, change, begin, end. One might characterize the whole of reality as a complex interconnecting web of interrelationships. Such a metaphor, of course, must be qualified by the awareness that relationships are living and not static as is a web.

Because of the complex nature of the human being as a psychophysical being who both thinks and feels, relations have to be understood with the same complexity. That is, all relations have some degree of the physical, the affective, the cognitive, in varying and often shifting measures. Thus, any relationship is itself a highly complicated reality, and can only be truly comprehended if all aspects are taken into account. Consequently, any representation of the whole of reality must take account of the complexity of relationships—their richness and their varying elements.

The process of human understanding is not only a matter of complex interrelations of physical, affective, and cognitive dimensions. Because the process is one of constant interaction, there is a temporal growth and progression in any person's knowing. That which one feels and understands from infancy and childhood is the foundation of that which one feels and understands as one grows older. Perceptions are interwoven to form increasingly more complex patterns of reality, with ever more nuanced and intricate images. Memory and expectations of the future expand the patterns, and depth and breadth of understanding increase. Time is the measure not of meaningless isolated changes, but of expanding insights into the whole.

Such is true for the individual and also for human beings as a community. As individuals increase in their own personal under-standings, perceptions, and relationships to reality, so also they share and integrate their own understandings with others to provide a more richly nuanced apprehension of the human condition. This process, which we call history, interweaves various stories to form an ever more complex and fluid whole. Individual members of communities with each other, communities with one another, nation with nation, culture with culture, intermingling of classes, religions, sexes, ages: the human story is constantly expanding in complexity to give a more complete and sensitive self-perception to the whole of human experience throughout time. As the stories are blended together, the significance of the human drama becomes more clear to humanity as such, and the human com-munity as a whole becomes more conscious of its place in the cosmic whole.

Evil and Fragmentation

While I have affirmed these vitally important insights I must also qualify them. The human experience which expresses a profound faith in the present goodness and future hope in the world's future also knows that expectations can be disappointed and futures can be de-spoiled. We continuously discover apparently unending dimensions to know, admire, respond to, and shape in our world; at the same time we find limits circumscribing our existences, and borders and endings which signal death and decay, with potential for total destruction. Even though we may affirm finitude and boundaries as good and proper, the human experience does not always happily respond to that limitation.[9]

On a cosmic level, the "death" of a star can cause massive destruction of other surrounding bodies through the loss of heat. What significance does such destruction have for the universe as a whole?

In the realm of nature, the same water which brings life to crops can cause, through drought or excess, the harvest to fail and plants to die. The story of evolution is not only a tale of success, but also of failure and death of individuals and species.[10]

In both individual and collective human life, some choices block off other possibilities. An individual who is primarily occupied with book-keeping and accounting will probably be relatively insensitive to social and interpersonal problems and issues, and persons especially aware of social needs are frequently impractical about the financial dimensions of complex socioeconomic concerns. Instead of forming a good team, often such persons are unable to communicate and work together.

Sometimes we, as thinking, desiring, and willing beings, experience the fragmentary nature of our own knowledge, perceptions, affections. We are only aware of some of those things of which we ought to be aware. Sometimes other human persons are opaque to us, and we misinterpret, reacting to others' language and physical expressions in a way that is quite different from their intentions. Sometimes as we put together ideas and insights in our process of cumulative knowing, through misapprehension we connect understandings improperly and wrongly because of the limits of our insights. The whole interpretation given to the world by individuals and groups may be wrong because of the limits of our ability to connect ideas.

Not only are we limited in our understandings and apprehensions of the world, and our universe itself is bound by limits which do not appear to fit any possible explanation of the whole which we can imagine, but we humans also experience a condition of willed evil. (To our knowledge this is a specifically human phenomenon, but that may be because of our inability to communicate directly with other living beings.) Not only are we ignorant and limited because of the sorts of beings we are, bound in time and space, but we do on occasion cooperate in ignorance, and will to do that which we ought not to do. Human history abounds with accounts of persons who have in some measure conspired in harming others, having refused to do the good that they were clearly obligated to do for others, and who have sometimes deliberately done evil to others, usually for their own individual benefit. Sometimes this evil affects individuals, and sometimes whole communities and groups of persons.[11]

Even though we may discern signs of the way reality is, and the way it would be if it were most fully developed according to its possibilities, a fundamental dimension of fragmentation remains in our own experience of life. Not only do we discover limits, and ignorance, but also self-deception and willful wrong in ourselves and in others. The world contains an element of "surd," unintelligibility, both intellectually and affectively.[12] Because of its nature one cannot explain this "surd"—fragmentation—because it does not make sense; it works at cross principles with the dynamic of wholeness. The tragedy of fragmentation is that the whole world is in one way or another involved in it, and we acting, thinking, loving beings share in the most destructive form of fragmentation. We are not only limited and restricted in our abilities and achievements but we also allow limitations to be destructive, and sometimes use them to harm others. We see no sign that this fundamental characteristic of human beings has changed throughout the course of history. If anything, as the insights and achievements of human beings ever increase, so the capability for destruction on an individual, community, global, and perhaps cosmic scale grows correspondingly.

By and large, contemporary feminists do not deal in any substantial way with the many dimensions of fragmentation in life. Limits are accepted and affirmed by some, such as Penelope Washbourn, and evil is generally regarded as the power of oppression in patriarchal society. Mary Daly regards the patriarchy as intrinsically evil, and all who do not participate in women's separatism share in that evil. By and large, feminists have chosen to focus on the good in women, whether it be according to the vision of witchcraft or the Christian invitation to partnership in creation. One can understand and applaud the need to accentuate the positive and to support the self-appraisal and efforts of women who have so often been overtly or covertly suppressed. What I would suggest here, however, is that the experience of fragmentation, not only as something which happens to me because of the inherent limits of my constitution and because of events occurring to me but also because of what I accept and do myself, is a common human experience. Recognizing a general description of evil as we experience it, we recognize that its degree, its scope, varies enormously from person to person, and is affected substantially by personal capabilities, sex, class, economic resources, etc. In the last chapter I will identify specific issues further; what is crucial for the moment is the acknowledgment of a common human experience of fragmentation within and without the psychophysical system, as a given of experience and also a product of one's choices.

Is there any reconciliation? Is all life an experience of a never-to-be-resolved struggle between the forces of fragmentation and the quest for wholeness? The "laws" of nature tell us that homeostasis is not an easily achieved state of rest, but a hard-won achievement. A contest between two opposing forces seeks a resolution. Is there any possibility of a perpetual standoff between life and death, change and permanence, energy and matter? All we know and experience tells us that reality is active, living, and that conditions seek resolution. Even if one conceives of an infinitely expanding universe, the movements of the universe are movements toward something, seeking dissolution, new changing combinations or recombinations. To expand the scope of the question about reconciliation does not answer the fundamental query about the relationship between wholeness and fragmentation.

If one chooses to assume that anything makes sense at all, the ultimate conclusion must be, I believe, that wholeness must in some sense triumph over fragmentation. I use these terms advisedly. Fragmentation and wholeness are not related to each other like yin and yang, light and dark. Wholeness cannot ultimately include fragmentation, because fragmentation is the destruction of wholeness; in the same way one cannot live in a relationship of mutual love with someone bent on destruction of the relationship. Fragmentation and wholeness are not complements, but opponents and contraries; fragmentation has nothing to give of itself, for it simply names that force which prevents creatures from becoming more fully themselves.[13] We do not know why fragmentation and evil exist. Because of their very nature as unintelligible forces we cannot know why, but we can assert that they ought not to negate existence, and that the fundamental dynamic animating the cosmos seeks to nurture, to restore, and to heal broken reality into wholeness.

We search for some principle of wholeness which is present in the world we experience and of which we are a part. If the power of healing is not somehow already present among us, how can we know it? Wholeness will not be produced by some extraneous reality, but through some power within, which is part of the whole, identified with it, and which moves it toward its fulfillment through an organic movement of growth. To expect a foreign agency invading the universe to enable it to become itself would be akin to reading a dog a psychology book to teach it not to bite strangers. At the same time, whatever principle we seek must also in some way differ from the universe we know. Otherwise there should be some signs that fragmentation is being overcome, both individually and corporately. However, there seems to be no convincing evidence of that. The fragility of the universe's growth toward wholeness remains constant in our history. Only the shape of the threats varies.

God, Christ, and Wholeness

Although I think one can argue that the dynamic of the universe toward wholeness is doomed and illusory, I have rejected that possibility because I think it reduces the quest for understanding to ultimate failure and the efforts of the uniting power of love to futility. Ultimately, I would insist on a basic assumption that everything must mean something, and find its significance and fulfillment in unity with all that is. Everything makes sense as part of a whole, or it makes no sense at all; all unites and grows as a whole, or there is no real growth and life at all, merely a passing illusion.

Because I assert this, I would submit that there must be some reality that can heal the fragmentation of the world and its inhabitants and move them toward wholeness. What I will explore in the next chapter is the Divine Reality as the source and power of wholeness, from which all comes and to which all moves. Following that, I will sketch a Christology which will present Christ as the agent of wholeness and reconciler of fragmentation in the world. I will suggest that this Christology contains within itself both the dimension of brokenness and alienation which must be healed, and the power of healing making all things one and whole. Christ is that unifier because he incorporates in the crucifixion the depths of the experience of fragmentation, and in the resurrection the transformation of that fragmentation into wholeness. The crucified and risen Christ richly expresses the dynamic movement toward wholeness that feminism seeks.

NOTES

1. Bernard Lonergan, *Insight: A Study of Human Understanding* (New York: Philosophical Library, 1957), xxviii.

2. Michael Polanyi, *Personal Knowledge: Towards a Post-Critical Philosophy* (New York: Harper & Brothers, 1958), 62.

3. Vine Deloria, *The Metaphysics of Modern Existence* (New York: Harper & Row, 1979).

4. Lonergan's *Insight* provides a very helpful analysis of the process of human knowing, which I am following in its general outlines. For a brief analysis of his ideas about epistemology which I think are relevant to our present quest, see Patricia Wilson, "Human Knowledge of God's Existence in the Theology of Bernard Lonergan," *The Thomist* 35 (April 1971): 259–75.

5. Caroline Merchant, *The Death of Nature: Women, Ecology, and the Scientific Revolution* (New York: Harper & Row, 1980), xvii.

6. For brief introductions to these developments, accessible to the layperson, see Thomas Kuhn, *The Essential Tension: Selected Studies in Scientific Tradi-*

tion and Change, 2d ed. (Chicago: Univ. of Chicago Press, 1977) and *The Structure of Scientific Revolutions* (Chicago: University of Chicago Press, 1970); Jacob Bronowski, *Science and Human Values* (New York: Harper & Row, 1965); George Gamov, *One Two Three . . . Infinity* (New York: Bantam Books, 1961); John Gribbin, *Time Warps* (New York: Delacorte Press/Eleanor Friede, 1979), esp. 3–65; Ian Barbour, *Issues in Science and Religion* (New York: Harper & Row, Harper Torchbooks, 1966, 1971), esp. 137–463.

7. As is immediately obvious, the outline I am sketching is related to that general movement called "process thought." For an introduction to process thought and its journey from philosophy to theology, see Alfred North Whitehead, *Process and Reality* (New York: Free Press, 1929, 1957) esp. 403–13; Charles Hartshorne, *A Natural Theology for Our Time* (LaSalle, Ill.: Court, 1967); Norman Pittenger's *Alfred North Whitehead* (Richmond, Va.: John Knox Press, 1969) has valuable insights about how Whitehead's philosophy is used by theologians; Peter Hamilton's *The Living God and the Modern World* (Philadelphia: United Church Press, 1967) provides a helpful basic introduction to the theology which has developed in process thought. What I will suggest as a constructive position will be far closer to the thought of Pierre Teilhard de Chardin. See his *The Phenomenon of Man* (New York: Harper & Row, 1965), *The Future of Man* (New York: Harper & Row, 1964), and *Hymn of the Universe* (New York: Harper & Row, 1965). For a helpful general introduction, see Henri de Lubac, *The Religion of Teilhard de Chardin* (London: William Collins Sons, 1967). Although there are significant relationships between Teilhard de Chardin's thought and process theology, the roots and certain key notions are substantially different.

8. One of the dangers of language is that we tend to assume that words always stand in a one-to-one correspondence to things ("reification"). Because I use words such as "body" and "spirit" does not mean that I think that there are discrete entities which correspond to the words. I do mean to indicate by these words the physical and spiritual aspects which I think can be distinguished in the human person, even though these aspects cannot and ought not to be separated. For a good introduction to the question, see James B. Nelson, *Embodiment: An Approach to Sexuality and Christian Ethics* (Minneapolis: Augsburg Pub. House, 1978).

9. The classical Thomistic tradition distinguished between physical and moral evil. Other divisions could be made. I have chosen to use the term "fragmentation" to designate both an experience which is part of the structure of the world as we know it, and also something which creatures assent to, desire, and sometimes will. The term fragmentation seems to me to be more descriptive of the phenomenon, at the same time that it indicates that fragmentation is not a good, if wholeness is the fruition of the world and its inhabitants.

10. A fascinating argument against the notion of a rationally comprehensi-

ble whole in which God is active is found in Raymond Nogar's *The Lord of the Absurd* (New York: Herder & Herder, 1966), in which is developed a Christology based on the very lack of coherence and continuity in the evolutionary process.

11. Margaret Fuller, in *Woman in the Nineteenth Century* (New York: W.W. Norton, 1971) wrote extensively of the wholeness of divine harmony for which the world was made and toward which it strives, and which is hindered by the oppression of women, blacks, Indians, because when a part is harmed, the whole suffers. See esp. pp. 19–30.

12. In *Insight,* 687–96, Lonergan uses the term "surd" to describe evil as unintelligibility, and the role of the "surd" as bringing one to the recognition of the need to seek some transcendent healing of the human condition.

13. My understanding of fragmentation is in this regard much the same as the Augustinian understanding of evil, which seems to me in this context more adequate than any other explanation.

CHAPTER 3

Feminism and Humanity

WHO IS A HUMAN?

Human knowing, as I have suggested, tells us a great deal about knowing but also about the person who does the knowing. Having explored in some depth a reconstruction of a Christian feminist epistemology, I now want to outline a theological anthropology, that is, the theology of being human. Based on their understanding of the way women relate to the world in knowing it, new descriptions of the human are being undertaken by the feminists. Radical feminists have insisted that male and female humanness is indeed radically different, if not theoretically, certainly in the reality of this world in which we actually live. Women are fundamentally good, they insist, though women are the victims of male oppression. Moreover, the foundation of values, and therefore of the ethical decision-making process for women, must be based on their own experience and not on artificially imposed patriarchal codes.

As must be obvious from my own suggestions about epistemology, such assertions are untenable in my opinion. I would propose, rather, a more inclusive theological anthropology. The point of departure is clear: How does one think about persons? Primarily as humans, or first as male or female?

Humanity: The One or the Many?

Perhaps because of their intense and justified preoccupation with one specific issue, that of sexism and oppression of women, many feminists begin by writing about persons primarily as male persons or female persons. Male persons are identified as the oppressors who have consciously or more often unconsciously lived in and promoted a social and religious system in which they perceived and presented themselves as normative humanity. Women were included as human sometimes, but they could never be certain just when. For example, consider the debate about the inclusiveness of the term "man." True as it is that in grammatical theory women were included in the generic term, it was almost always by way of exception, and women could never be sure when they were included and when not.[1] Examples of "men" were almost invariably male, so that women and men were encouraged to believe that man, in fact though not in theory, means "male person." The measure of "man" was maleness.

This little linguistic example is merely a concrete example of a cultural bias which almost totally pervades human societies. Consequently we should register no surprise when women, conscious of the oppression and exclusion to which they had been subject, focus on their femaleness, uphold it, remark on it, praise it, and identify it specifically in order to discover its true depths. At the same time, emphasis on the separation of persons into male and female as the initial reference is a major mistake. It seems to me much more useful, and, as I will suggest, more faithful to both Scripture and the fundamental insights of feminism, to begin by assuming a common humanity. To begin one's considerations of humanity by dividing the human race into male and female is to start as the Victorian who spoke condescendingly of women as the weaker sex. One merely reverses the order of excellence.

The importance of insisting on the essential unity of humanity cannot be overemphasized. How ironic it is that the most vigorous proponents of a binary theory of humanity are the feminist separatists and male opponents of women's equality in church or society. These two extremes agree only that male and female humanity are not the same. I suggest, however, that the fundamental commonness of humanity encompassing male and female is not only an observation of the social sciences, it is an absolute necessity for an inclusive theology.

There is a fundamental consensus in contemporary scientific anthropology and psychology that the most fundamental category of humanity *is* humanity.[2] The division of persons into male and female is significant, but it is one category among many. To categorize human beings into male and female, prior to an assertion of their common humanity, invites sexism and oppression, whether of the male or female mode. A doctrine of "separate but equal" can no more be put into effect between males and females than between black and white, and finds no support in the mainline of scientific study.

Sex is one factor among many qualifying our common humanity. Important a factor as it is, it is not determinative. For instance, individual psychophysical variations among females, and at different stages of their lives, at least rival the differences between the sexes. Height, body shape, age, class, and nationality are also shaping factors. In Aristotelian terminology, sex and other aspects of the person are accidents modifying essential humanity.

Biblical and theological analysis is even more emphatic about the essential unity of humanity.[3] Even the biblical passages most susceptible to sexist interpretation assert that in relationship to God women and men are equal; God hears the prayers of both, speaks to both; both are invited to be part of God's people and to partake of eternal life in God. Restrictions on women, of which there are many in the Hebrew Bible and in the New Testament, refer to earthly society. The key interpretive question for the Christian then becomes: how much does the end-time break into the present? How much ought the here-and-now to be like the way it ought to be, the ideal to be sought after in this life? Although many responses have been offered over the course of the church's history, it seems to me that only one response is admissible: the reign of God, with its justice, peace, love, and truth, should be actualized on this earth. The living of the Christian life is a constant effort to bring heaven and earth together, to make the ideal actual. Perfect harmony will never be known in this life, but one must continually search for it. Thus the life of individual Christians, the life of the Church, and the life of a Christianly animated society must always seek to ensure that "in Christ there is neither Jew nor Greek, slave nor free, male nor female" (Gal. 3:28).

To be baptized into Christ and admitted to the Lord's table affirms a unity of humanity which already exists, and creates and recreates an increasing unity in Christ. Such unity in Christ is not an oppressive or leveling unity, but one in which, because we all are children of God and brothers and sisters of each other, individual gifts and differences are allowed to develop according to the gifts given, not because of stereotyped patterns. Unity grows from a community of persons, who are diverse and yet have been brought together in a new configuration because they have been joined together with other persons in one organic whole.

The Pauline letters develop the metaphor of the body of Christ to express the living tension between the ordered life of the church and the enthusiastic expression of the many individual charisms or gifts of the

Holy Spirit. In Paul's theology, the order of common life in the body of Christ must be equally weighed with the expression of charisms such as teaching, administering, encouraging, and others given for the service of the community. Diversity is a value, serving the community's life together in Christ; but the common life ought to nurture the multitude of charisms given to the various individuals. All find their unity in Christ, whose Spirit acts in varied ways to build the Christian community (1 Cor. 12:1–30; Rom. 12:4–8; Eph. 4:4–16; Col. 3:12–15).

As a Christian I must affirm that humanity is one, and at the same time as varied as each of the persons who are called human. Females and males were created after the image of God, and the same God is imaged in each of them (Gen. 1:26–27). Each person is a variation on the infinite possibilities of the divine imaged in humanity. Humanity encompasses oneness and rich diversity, of which femaleness and maleness are two components. Through its encompassing and nurturing of differences within a common unity humanity is an important force of coherence within creation.

Although the notion of human being as microcosm cannot be stretched to some of the extremes of Gnostic or Kabbalistic speculation, at the same time it contains several useful ideas which were popular among some theologians of the early church, and later writers who were influenced by them.[4] Gregory of Nyssa reasons in the manner of rabbis and Christian theologians who went before him, asserting that human beings were created last in the order of creation to indicate their relationship to it. According to Gen. 1:26, humans ought to rule over creation as God rules over them, rather than being permitted by God to dominate and despoil the earth. An evermore intimate and internal relationship prevails between humans and the rest of creation. God created human beings last because human beings are related to every living creature. They grow physically as do plants; they sense and feel as do the animals. (For Gregory, rocks and stone, which he did not consider to be living beings, did not figure in this analysis.) At the same time that they are like the plant and animal world, human beings also share some of the characteristics of God and the angels: they think, know, and will. For Gregory, both males and females share those characteristics.

Body and soul are not opposed to each other, as two warring forces, but the soul is the mirror of the divine beauty and truth. The body and material world are in turn the "mirror of the mirror," the reflection of the divine beauty as expressed in the spiritual realm. Such a variation of the "chain of being" underscored the orderly connection between the different versions of the divine goodness and beauty in finite creation. Humanity's unique position is that it is intrinsically both spiritual and material, an unbreakable unity holding together the two realms as one. In its very created nature humanity concretely manifests the unbreakable unity of creator and creation. Its various possibilities reflect the richness of the possible combinations of created being. At the same time the firm unity of humanity rests on its oneness as the royal community called by God to lead all creation in expressing its worship of God.[5]

Later theologians adapted these insights in different contexts. For instance, Jonathan Edwards, the eighteenth-century American Puritan, wrote eloquently of the role of humanity as the link between the lower visible creation and the divine reality within a predestinarian context. Whereas Gregory of Nyssa stressed human freedom, Edwards regarded God as the sole directing force in the return of the cosmos to God through humanity.[6] In the twentieth century Pierre Teilhard de Chardin expressed this faith from a perspective clothed in the scientific theory of evolution. Teilhard de Chardin suggested that humanity represents a stage in the development of the cosmos, its coming to consciousness and its enfolding on itself in the sphere of cosmic self-awareness, the noosphere. Planetary self-awareness exists not for itself, in Teilhard de Chardin's opinion, but as the means for the world to find its fulfillment in God, the Omega point.[7]

In diverse ways, each of these theologians shares a fundamental insight into the understanding of humanity. The human race is not simply an aggregate of individuals lumped together through some accident of biological history; humanity is part of the living whole which we call the cosmos, and the cosmos itself realizes its fullest individual and corporate reality through its relationship to God. Humanity occupies a key position because of its ability to understand and to love, to acknowledge the created reality of the world, its participation in the world, and at the same time its innate affinity for the divine life.

At the same time that each being in the world has its own integrity, each and every one finds its ultimate fulfillment in the service of God, according to one's own capacity. Through humanity the world can consciously know and love the God who created and sustains it. At the same time, because of its affinity to God, in its longing to love and to know the cosmos more profoundly, in its ability to care for and to nurture the creation, humanity expresses God's concern and creative passion to the world. As embodied selves, humans use their own material selves to exercise the divine love in the visible creation. At the same time that humanity has a divine nurturing responsibility to creation, it also has a priestly obligation to represent creation before God. As priests, human beings praise and adore God as the conscious, articulate representatives of the universe.[8]

To assert that female and male persons are radically different, as some feminists do, or that they should develop distinctively different personalities, would create divisions in the role of humanity in its cosmic responsibilities. The unity of humanity in relation of God and the creation would be destroyed. Some opponents of women's ordination have even suggested that an appropriate symbolism would be for women to exercise a nurturing role toward creation, and men to be God's representatives to the world. Such an approach is not only arrogant, but unscriptural.

The Bible is unquestioningly clear that all humans *as* humans bear responsibility for the created order (Gen. 1:26–30). Furthermore, the people of God in particular are called as a people to these responsibilities. Despite later cultic exclusion of women from public roles in worship, biblical religion does not speak about male and female prayer, or discriminate between women's and men's hearing of the Word. The Scriptures focus on the responsibility of humanity toward God and creation. The unity of humanity is essential if humanity is to fulfill its vocation in creation. Any feminism which does not also begin with an assumption of one human race, composed of female and male, black, white, yellow, short, tall, and so forth, each equally human and not bound by preconceived roles, is not compatible with the Christian faith. At the same time, Christian faith which does not insist on the fundamental equality of all human persons is not only not feminist but also not truly Christian.

The Complexity of Humanity

Having insisted on the unity of the human race, one must also recognize the extreme complexity of that same humanity. Each human person is the nexus of a complex of factors which staggers the imagination. Composed of elements as basic as those in the ocean water, and subject to the same sorts of sensations as a dog or a squirrel, we also can imagine realms of outer space and fourth-dimensional geometry. We are in turn irascible and kind, greedy and yet self-sacrificing enough to give up our lives for others, strong and weak, nurturing and yet rigidly ordering things and people. Amazingly, each human person—to some degree—may embrace each of these characteristics and more, in different ways, at different times, and sometimes at one and the same time.[9]

Human beings come in different sizes and shapes, with varying characteristics and desires, shaped by and having responded to a variety of experiences in quite distinct ways, in varying bodies, some male, and some female. Unquestionably maleness and femaleness, with potential for human reproduction and sexual relationships, are highly significant factors in the process of being human, although not determinative ones.[10] To settle on maleness or femaleness as being the single most important aspect of a person, overriding even common humanity, misses our common human characteristics.

If one is seeking to understand humanity and its role, it is more to the point to identify fundamental traits in all human beings, which are exercised differently by different persons. Two elements are constitutive of all human persons, however. First, a person is one who is self-possessed, self-focused, self-conscious, capable of loving, willing, knowing, and capable of making decisions. To be a person involves not only internal psychic activity, but also knowing that she or he is the center of such activity; a person is to some degree self-reflexive. Self-awareness is not only expressed internally in thought, but also in every aspect of the person's being, especially in speech, that most ethereal physical expression of mental life. The second characteristic of the person is equally important in individual and community life. A person is one who is also capable of coming forth from the self, transcending the boundaries of the ego without losing the "I," finding fulfillment in the other as well as in the self, able to be empathetic with both the self and others.[11]

A person is at one and the same time self-possessing and self-giving, self-centered and self-transcending. One who is fully a person is not obsessed with self to the point of excluding concern for others and using them to serve his or her own ends. At the same time, she or he is not so other-directed and attentive to give to others, serve them, and find satisfaction by filling their needs that she or he is void of self-centeredness, the consciousness of the "I" who is dedicated to others. These dimensions of the person are not opposed to each other, but are essential polarities which must be both active and interacting for a person to be truly human.

Rather than being united in a single notion of self, these two characteristics are frequently separated along lines of sexual identity. Males are identified as those who are possessive, self-possessed, and self-directed, while women are characterized as finding their satisfaction in serving others, loving them, and losing their own sense of self. Sexual stereotypes, if viewed from this perspective, not only destroy the unity of the human race but also fragment humanity by dividing the integrity of the very person. Not only is the whole of humanity damaged as a unity, but each individual person is cut to the heart as to her or his identity. Males are encouraged to surrender their sense of self-transcendence, perceptions of values, love and self-sacrifice for others; those are women's activities. Females are told that their fulfillment comes in serving others without any regard for themselves or their own desires.

The search for a more holistic understanding of the person is an issue at the heart of this book. The bifurcation of male and female needs to be redressed. No one is fully a person who is not both self-possessing and also self-giving/self-transcending, whether that person be male or female.

This complex analysis of the person becomes even more complex when one acknowledges that what has just been described is an abstract, idealized description of what human beings can and ought to be like. Missing is the dimension of reality which we described in our exploration of epistemology. In the real world persons are indeed complex, consisting of many factors, beings who are both self-possessed and self-giving. But because the balance is complicated and delicate, it can easily become warped, damaged, or destroyed.

One element or factor can so overweigh the others that the balance and harmony is lost. Such a loss of equilibrium can be quite destructive for the person or for others. Not only does this imbalance affect our knowing process and our way of perceiving the world but it also may damage one's personality.

Valerie Saiving has observed that Western theology has recognized sin according to male models, accepting Augustine's dictum that sin is pride, and that the antidote for it is humility and a self-giving attitude.

Unhappily, she notes, that emphasis has insured that women, who have had the self-possessed side of their natures suppressed already, are intimidated by a double dose of prescribed submissiveness. Advocacy of such submissiveness is inappropriate to the sinful tendency to surrender or relinquish the self as well as one's sense of self-worth and centeredness through a wholly other-centered sense.[12]

Although I do not concur with Saiving's identification of certain intrinsic male and female characteristics, she clearly underlines the destructive tendencies of human stereotyping, and also the way in which differing distortions of human personhood emerge from certain societally prescribed expectations and socially determined boundaries.

In developing a Christian anthropology one must assert that a fundamentally good human nature, as we know it in all its various manifestations, tends toward self-destruction, harm toward others, self-deception, and even the twisting of the good into that which is less good and sometimes very harmful. All of our human characteristics which ought to work together to such good for the self and love towards others become twisted and fragmented. The extent of our destructiveness ranges from the little white lie which mildly misleads others to the vindictive destruction of masses of people. The source of all such evil is this same distortion of the self. Assuredly this is what the Scriptures meant by sin. The theological treatments of original sin and actual sin are attempts, of course, to explain this incomprehensible aspect of the human condition.[13] The most puzzling matter, however, is that such fragmentation—sin—seems to be a part of our lives from cradle to grave, from infancy to death. The permutations of our sinfulness change; our tendencies remain constantly present.[14]

The distortion and disharmony within us and around us remind us of our need for healing. Because we are fragmented and out of balance at the very core of human selfhood, our healing must transform and enable the entire person to become more whole and self-integrated. The person must be empowered to become both self-possessed and self-centered as well as self-transcending and self-giving. Only if these two essential polarities of being human are integrated and exercised is a person human in a way that can shape all other human variables into a psycho-sexual-spiritual whole. Such healing and growth is a highly complex and lifelong process, but essential to the health of humanity, both individual and corporate.

GROUNDING HUMAN VALUES:
A NEW ETHICS

We have previously noted that some feminists tend to ground the decision-making and knowing process in the experience of individual women, and perhaps in the community of sisterhood. By and large, however, Christian feminists insist that ethics should begin with a reinterpretation from a holistic and feminist perspective. Women's experience, they contend, will indeed bring new insights and new dimensions to bear on the Christian faith and theology. If this is to be the case, what will this mean for ethics? Is a proper ethical action one that makes an individual woman feel fulfilled? Is it one that gives the most benefit to the sisterhood, the community? What is the foundation of values in a Christian feminist theology?

The issue here is similar to the one faced by proponents of liberation and black theologies, due to the focus on the experience of one particular group as the prism through which various theological issues are refracted.[15] If one posits or promotes "the good" of the group—the special concern of a specific theology—as the foundation of values, then the standard for making decisions is clear: "the good" is determined by the benefit derived by that particular group, which is the focus of that specific theology. Thus Marxist ethics is extremely influential in, and sometimes almost identical with, the search for value in liberation theology. Because the interpretation of society and the analysis of the human condition are often so influenced by Marxism, so too is the ethical process. A similar phenomenon can be noted in feminist theology: inasmuch as the analysis of society and interpretation of the human being rest on radical or reformist feminist foundations, so also will the ethics.

My own constructive approach is that of a reformist feminist, and depends on an understanding of the human being which rests on a unified humanity and an insistence that sexuality is one factor among many in the composition of the human person, and not by itself radically constitutive of the person. Consequently, the ethics which I propose must arise from a focus not primarily on woman's experience or any other specific sort of person's experience. Experience is not, as Paul Tillich most ably insists, a particular content but the medium through which reality becomes known to and appropriated by us.[16] To base a theology on women's experience, or blacks', or Native Americans', or white males' is to base a theology on a point of view that is by definition limited. One might even define experience, in our human context, as limitation. Through one's experience certain realities, from a wide range of possible realities, are incorporated into one's own mental world as significant and meaningful. At the same time that "experience" signifies the limitation of any given person, it also enables the person, through inference from others' accounts of their own experiences, empathy, and concern, to open up one's personal horizons to the reality of others, and to incorporate these various understandings into a greater whole than one's own narrow perception of reality.

Although awareness of one's experience, one's point of view, is essential for a critical consciousness of what one is doing in constructing a theological approach, nevertheless one needs a broader base than one person's or even one group's perspective. To gain new insights today, one needs to take into account a variety of perspectives, and find a firmer, more plausible base for theology. That base must involve both the whole human community, not just a part of that community, and the God who is the source of that whole. Therefore, the foundation of our ethics must be firmly rooted in the entire human community *and* in the divine, or the foundation itself will be so shaky and uncertain that the new structures may not fare better than the prejudiced system we hope to replace.

A reformist feminist theology insists that the foundation of future constructive theology should incorporate the feminist concern for human wholeness. It must do so within the context of the theological affirmations about the unity of humanity and the fragmentation which we each experience in our individual selves and in corporate life of the human community—our world. Our emphasis on wholeness and a recognition of our brokenness is not peripheral, but lies at the heart of ethical concerns. In our movement toward inclusiveness, we should also take account of global and cosmic issues. Our humanity is not an isolated unit; rather it is an integral part of the ecosystem of the universe. If our fundamental relationship lies in human unity, then *all* values and decisions which are made by humans must take account of the whole. Such decision-making involves not only a balancing and weighing of many factors respecting individual diversity but also the complexity of our interrelationships. Consequently, any decision which particularizes, which divides, which in any way damages the integrity of the unity of humanity is wrong because falsely grounded.

Just as it is wrong to pay lower wages to various minorities on racist grounds, so it is wrong to treat women on sexist grounds. As Margaret Fuller pointed out in the nineteenth century, it is morally wrong to do anything that artificially restricts the capabilities or the expression of the abilities of any person, male or female, red, black, yellow, or white, because to do so is to distort and damage the health of the whole human community. At the same time, individuals and communities must make their decisions with a view to maximizing the good of the community in light of their individual capabilities. So, for instance, a wife or husband is not free simply to move wherever career possibilities bid; rather, the effects on the family unity must be sensitively balanced before the risks are taken. On a broader scale, the need for arming a nation must be balanced not only in light of the balance of power among nations, and the general effect on the "arms race," but also in light of effects on the economy and the social stability of the nations involved, and eventually of the world. While such a decision-making process seems complex (and on one level it is), at the same time such a process draws attention to the unity and interrelationship of the whole global character of the community in Christ.

One of the most significant contributions that such a reformist feminist ethics could make to the discipline of ethics would be to renew the sense of "the common good," the notion that all human-made decisions must attend not only to the individual but also to the good of the whole. It is never possible to know precisely what "the common good" is, because the notion of "the common good" in this life is oriented to the "ultimate" good. I cannot, for instance, say precisely what the economic "common good" of the United States is at any one given time, because the variables and relationships to other nations are always changing. The notion of "common good" does not and cannot prescribe a detailed program. It can, however, point in the direction of ideals toward which we ought to be striving, means which should be employed, and higher priority of certain goods over others in perspective of the whole. The "common good" lures and prods us on toward what ought to be, the peace and unity of the whole.

We here and now are able to derive a real, though partial, sense of what that harmony of the whole might be, and that vision enables us to aim toward the good of the whole. In our labors toward "the common good" we are encouraged to overcome those divisions which our fragmentation nurtures, including those based on sex distinctions. We are inspired to unite ever more closely as one mutually loving community, so that repression and oppression may decline as the possibilities for each person in the whole are actualized. Even though we recognize that our efforts will always be deficient, nonetheless we acknowledge that our decisions and actions ought to be based on these considerations.[17]

FROM THEORY TO ACTUALITY

Here we have outlined a reformed Christian anthropology, one that is in dialogue with Christian feminist concerns. We have recognized in ourselves a drive toward wholeness and completeness in community; at the same time we feel within us a fragmentation and disharmony which cries out for healing. Within this context, we will address the central Christian theological issue: who is the Christ? This is the one whom the Christian claims as not only the healer of all which is amiss but also the source and the goal of cosmic wholeness.

NOTES

1. For a general discussion of the question of inclusive language, see Casey Miller and Kate Swift, *Words and Women* (New York: Doubleday, Anchor Books, 1976); for an introduction to specifically religious issues, see Marianne Sawicki, *Faith and Sexism* (New York: Seabury Press, 1979), 7–17.

2. Marianne Micks, *Our Search for Identity* (Philadelphia: Fortress Press, 1982), surveys opinions about the issue. For a brief popular anthropological treatment of the theme of the unity of humanity, see Richard Leakey and Roger Lavin, *Origins* (New York: E.P. Dutton, 1977), 230–37.

3. For an analysis of the sources, Leonard Swidler, *Biblical Affirmations of Women* (Philadelphia: Westminster Press, 1979), 75–355; Paul Jewett, *The Ordination of Women* (Grand Rapids: Wm. B. Eerdmans, 1980), 4–12; Krister Stendahl, *The Bible and the Role of Women* (Philadelphia: Fortress Press, Facet Books, 1966).

4. Plato, *Timaeus* (Baltimore: Penguin Books, 1965), 56–57, 118–19. For an example from the early church, see Gregory of Nyssa, *On the Soul and Resurrection*, 441–42; *On the Making of Man*, 394–96 in Nicene and Post-Nicene Fathers, 2nd series, vol. V (Grand Rapids: Wm. B. Eerdmans, 1976). For Kabbalistic developments, see Gershom Sholem, *On the Kabbalah and Its Symbolism* (New York: Schocken Books, 1969), 128, 167, 169, and *Major*

Trends in Jewish Mysticism (New York: Schocken Books, 1941), 268–69; an introductory article with bibliography is found in Donald Levy's entry in the *Encyclopedia of Philosophy*, s.v. "Macrocosm and Microcosm."

5. Gregory of Nyssa, *On the Making of Man*, Nicene and Post-Nicene Fathers, 2nd series, V: 398–99.

6. Jonathan Edwards, "Dissertation on the End for Which the World Was Created," in *The Works of Jonathan Edwards* (Edinburgh: Banner of Truth Trust, 1974), 1:94–121.

7. Pierre Teilhard de Chardin, *The Phenomenon of Man: The Divine Millieu* (New York: Harper & Brothers, 1960).

8. Robert Capon, *An Offering of Uncles* (New York: Crossroad, 1982). Capon describes in theologically rich but nontechnical language the priestly dimension of all human existence.

9. I do not intend to deal with the vexing issues of when a person becomes human, or about the humanity of seriously brain-damaged persons. For a review of the complexities of the arguments, see Joseph Fletcher, *Humanhood: Essays in Biomedical Ethics* (Buffalo: Prometheus, 1979) and Paul Ramsey, *Ethics at the Edges of Life: Medical and Legal Intersections* (New Haven, Conn.: Yale Univ. Press, 1978).

10. Margaret Mead's excellent *Male and Female* (New York: Wm. Morrow, 1975) observes that the roles assigned to men and women in various cultures differ substantially and are sometimes contradictory if one assumes absolute differences. Her observation that there are distinct sex roles and that higher value is always attached to male activity sets the issue in a context of power, rather than sexual determinism. Much contemporary research in psychology and social development centers on differences between male and female character, e.g., Carol Gilligan's *A Different Voice: Psychological Theory and Women's Development* (Cambridge, Mass.: Harvard Univ. Press, 1982). Emphasis is on diverse ways of actualizing common humanity and ways men and women struggle differently in our society with common values.

11. The definition of person has a complex philosophical and theological history. An introduction to some of the issues and their history may be found in *An Encyclopedia of Theology: The Concise Sacramentum Mundi* (New York: Seabury Press, 1975), s.v. "person." Edith Stein's *On the Problem of Empathy* (The Hague: Martinus Nijhoff, 1970) is especially helpful in showing how personal relationships are constitutive of the self.

12. See the ground-breaking article by Valerie Saiving, in *Womanspirit Rising*, ed. Carol Christ and Judith Plascow (New York: Harper & Row, 1979). Saiving's article, "The Human Situation: A Feminine View," pp. 25–42.

13. Karl Rahner's entry in *Encyclopedia of Theology*, s.v. "original sin." A helpful introduction to the scriptural and traditional interpretations of original sin is found in Herbert Haag's *Is Original Sin in Scripture?* (New York: Sheed and Ward, 1969).

14. For an exploration from a more psychological perspective, see Karl Menninger, *Whatever Happened to Sin?* (New York: Hawthorn, 1973).

15. See Gustavo Gutierrez, *A Theology of Liberation: History, Politics and Salvation* (Maryknoll, N.Y.: Orbis Books, 1973) and Jon Sobrino, *Christology at the Crossroads* (Maryknoll, N.Y.: Orbis Books, 1978).

16. Paul Tillich, *Systematic Theology* (Chicago: Univ. of Chicago Press, 1967), 1:40–46.

17. Patricia Wilson-Kastner, "Contemporary Feminism and the Christian Doctrine of the Human," *Word and World* 2 (Summer 1982): 234–42.

CHAPTER 4

Roots of the Problem in Christology

FROM AN INCLUSIVE TO AN EXCLUSIVE CHRISTOLOGY

Now that an inclusive epistemology and anthropology has been explored, the original challenge of the radical feminists appears even more insistent. How can those who insist on community and wholeness worship, venerate, or even pay any attention to the male Christ figure? The question is particularly acute because Christ has been used in the course of history as a symbol to justify male dominance in the church and society. Here I want to elucidate why feminism and Christology are not incompatible. To do so, I first intend to investigate some developments in Christian theology about Christ which contributed to the denigration of women. Once some of these unfortunate evolutions in Christian thought are identified and explained briefly, I will outline an agenda for a reconstruction of a more inclusive Christology.

The development of christological doctrine in the early church is an exceedingly complex and tortuous tale. Several centuries of ferment and conflict yielded an enormous amount of literature—of a controversial, apologetic, and didactic nature—and an even greater amount of scholarship about and analysis of the developments.[1] For our purposes the vexing issue is how Christianity—in four or five centuries—moved *from* an egalitarian Jesus of the gospels who accepted women as human beings on a par with men, *to* an exclusivistic Christ, one who was portrayed by the church with increasing frequency as a figure of male excellence. Here I can only sketch an ever so brief overview of this transformation.

Jesus in His Times

In Jesus' time the position and status of women varied greatly according to class, economic level, and the land where one lived. Although

71

research has been done into the Judaism of Jesus' age, one would like to know more about the status of women. The general picture of women in Palestinian Judaism is of a class generally subordinate to men. Although there are a few exceptional individual women of achievement, because women were in practice and theory not bound to the fulfillment of any precepts of the Law, nor to the study of it, they normally did not have access to the knowledge of the Law which gave status and a sense of value in the Jewish community.[2]

In the perspective of his time, Jesus' treatment of women was un-condescendingly attentive. His relatively frank and open relationships with them are quite remarkable.[3] This characteristic of Jesus' ministry needs to be underscored because his stance was preserved in the Gospels, those documents written and collected in the church as the canon for identifying those aspects of Jesus' life. At least in the beginning, the church must have felt that Jesus' attitude toward women was an appropriate model for its own life as well. Jesus' relationships with women were within the bounds of Jewish Law, as we can infer from his enemies' failure to attribute any impropriety to him, even when they were seeking to entrap him. Nonetheless, his attentiveness to women as people was rare in the context of his culture and remark-ably sensitive.

What Jesus does not do is almost as remarkable as what he does do. He does not proclaim a part of his gospel to women and most of it to men. He teaches women as well as men. In the famous Mary and Martha story, for instance, Mary is assumed to be sitting at Jesus' feet and listening to him teach as did any other disciple, and Jesus behaves as though there is no question of her right to do so. Jesus never says anything demeaning to women, trivializes them, or praises their special "women's contribution." In his own presentation of himself, he com-pares himself to a mother hen; in describing his mission he assumes the attributes of Wisdom, the feminine personification of the divine activ-ity; and in one of his parables he compares God to a housewife seeking a lost coin. Given his membership in a patriarchal society, the Jesus in the Gospels is remarkably nonsexist and inclusive in his relations with women.

In the world to which Christianity spread as it moved out of Palestine, the legal and social position of women was quite mixed. For instance, in Greece the rights of women were very limited, whereas in Rome the legal standing of women, with rights to own and dispose of property, had improved dramatically over the two or three centuries before Christ. Even though women in Rome had certain rights in law, however, they were firmly excluded from government and allowed a very limited place in religious leadership. At the beginning of its movement out into the Greco-Roman world, Christianity seemed to follow that lead of Jesus in his treatment of women. Many of the organizers and leaders of the early church were women—Lydia, Phoebe the deacon, and Junias the apostle, if one accepts the name as feminine. Certainly the Acts of the Apostles reflects a very active participation of women in the spread of Christianity, not only as listeners and followers, but also as leaders.

In the Bible itself we can trace a change from the first days of the church and the grand proclamation of Paul in Galatians (3:28), that in Christ there is neither male nor female, but all are one in Christ, to the much more restrictive legislation of the pastoral epistles. Paul himself appears to have worked well with women in his missionary work (Rom. 16:1–3; Acts 18:18, 26), recognized their leadership (1 Cor. 16:19; Acts 16:14–15), and assumes women's right to speak out in the assembly (1 Cor. 11:4). Unquestionably his early women hearers, usually women who were either Jewish or Gentiles sympathetic to Judaism, would have welcomed his message, which seemed to offer the fulfillment of the Jewish Law and its ethics. It also provided an attractive freedom for women. But already, by the third quarter of the first century, the acceptance of women as equal human persons in the church was being challenged (Col. 3:18, 1 Tim. 2:12, 1 Pet. 3:1–2). The subordination of women to men in marriage was being advocated in the church; no more striking affirmations of women's equality with men ring from the Scriptures. As the church became more organized and hierarchical, the place of women was being moved toward the periphery.

THE CULTURAL DILEMMA OF EARLY CHRISTIANITY

What happened? How do we explain the discrepancy between Jesus' life and teachings as the church preserved them, and the way in which the church so quickly fell away from Jesus' ideals and behavior, even within a few years of his death and resurrection? Dorothy L. Sayers eloquently describes the problem:

Perhaps it is no wonder that the women were first at the Cradle and last at the Cross. They had never known a man like this Man—there has never been such another. . . . Nobody could possibly guess from the words and deeds of Jesus that there was anything "funny" about women's nature. But we might easily deduce it from His contemporaries, and from His prophets before Him, and from His Church to this day. Women are not human; let them say what they like, we will not believe it, though One rose from the dead.[4]

Why did things so develop? No simple answer is available, but one or two crucial factors affected the process of development. One is the interaction between the environment of the Greco-Roman world and the religious and ethical standards of the early Christian community. Of course one must be aware of and acknowledge the complexities of the cultural world of the early Christian community. The legal and social status of Cappadocian women was not necessarily that of urban Roman women, and there were also significant distinctions between upper- and lower-class women. However, there are certain broad generalizations which one can make with validity if one wishes to account for trends over a long period.

Rigorous moral standards were characteristic of early Christian communities. The Christian community in the first few centuries insisted on a stringent moral code. Such insistence grew from commitment of the community's own interpretation of the demands of the gospel on everyday life. It was also influenced by the standard charge raised in classical antiquity about any new religion (that it was characterized by sexual license and orgiastic behavior). Probably, it also emerged from a desire to ensure that the early Christians understood themselves as set apart from the world which opposed them. In and of itself, to deemphasize women and men as sexual beings *could have* resulted in a centering on the thinking and willing capacities of persons as part of a common humanity—a shift very helpful to women. Unhappily this concern for sexual morality, combined with growing ascetical tendencies, served to suppress women even further.

Asceticism

The development of asceticism itself is an extremely complex and difficult phenomenon to account for and to understand to our satisfaction. Let us here examine the attitude toward women in the ascetical movement. As far back as its pre-Christian origins, one can discern two conflicting tendencies: because the body is subordinated to the spirit, and overt expressions of sexuality ought to be suppressed, male and female are equal in mental capability and thus equally human in the ascetical life style. On the other hand, women are identified with the body, the lower principle, and with sexuality. Therefore, they are a perennial danger to themselves and the men whom they may tempt, and for these reasons can never be regarded as equal to males.[5]

The relative importance in influence and numbers of ascetics in the church varied greatly over the centuries. In the early church one can document a significant rise in the third and fourth centuries, a phenomenon not unrelated to the urge toward withdrawal from society among the educated classes in the latter Empire. One can identify two differing styles of monasticism: one, the educated withdrawal for a contemplative life, the style of monasticism which produced literature; the other, the popular lower-class endeavor which specialized in spiritual power and deeds of holiness. Women played a significant role in the total monastic movement, and much more needs to be said about the "desert mothers,"[6] as well as their more educated sisters. But despite the significant participation of women in ascetical movements in various forms in the early church, an ambivalent attitude toward women remained very much a part of their theological and devotional literature. By the fourth century the most positive attitude one might hope for would be an assertion of women's equal spiritual abilities combined with a clear recognition that equality was a spiritual anticipation of the heavenly condition, and that it had no bearing on the present structure of church and society.[7]

Despite women's significance in the ascetical movement, much ambiguity and ambivalence about their true role in the church remained. The theoretical cause of this attitude lies deeply rooted in the intense dualism which pervaded both pagan and Christian Greco-Roman society. Rising out of Greek philosophical and religious attitudes, with probable influence from India and other parts of the Orient, the Platonists, Pythagoreans, and most other Greeks and Romans were exceedingly suspicious of the body. The body was of matter, that which was lower than spirit, and if the spirit were going to be worthy of and know the truth it needed to be purified of various lower tendencies.

One should be aware of the many nuances of various schools at differing stages in the development of the diverse groups, the ways their views were accepted into popular religious culture, and the process whereby Christian groups and thinkers incorporated these assumptions. The picture of the development of asceticism is highly complex and multiform. Overall, however, ascetical literature reflects an exceedingly negative attitude toward women. We do not know what women ascetics of this period may have thought, because their writings have not been preserved; we might infer, however, from the absence of records of significant conflict, that women may have believed some of the male ascetics' assertions about them, or perhaps they simply chose to ignore their male colleagues.

Because ascetics were not interested in the niceties of philosophical theory, but in the practices of purification leading to a further life of prayer with God, they were frequently uncompromisingly hostile toward women. Women were the embodiment, the personification, of the physical, the reproductive functions, and the sexual attraction of men and women for each other. Consequently bodies in general and women in particular were quite dangerous. Of course, such an attitude in literature assumes that ascetics are male and women are excluded, or that the values of asceticism revolve around male needs.

The tenor of these attitudes toward women and the physical—in the crucial period in which classical Christology was developing—ranges from the ambivalent to the highly negative, with the negative dominating. A concrete demonstration of this negative attitude is represented in the change in the types of women even acknowledged in writing preserved for us by ecclesiastics and ascetics during the first few centuries. In second-century literature one can read about various categories of women: the widows, virgins, young women, married women raising families, married and unmarried women studying and practicing the faith. In reading the fifth-century church fathers one would think that not many women were left in the church: occasional empresses and princesses, virgins, widows, and married women just waiting to get rid of their husbands so they might devote themselves to asceticism.[8] Wishful thinking as that may have been, it illustrates the attitude toward women among influential hierarchical and ascetic leaders, who directly or indirectly taught the masses of Christian men and women.

This attitude not only affected the way women as persons were treated in the early church; it also shaped significantly the ways in which

Christology was formulated and how Christ's redemptive activity toward humans was expressed. To appreciate some of its significance I want to center on two questions. Is Jesus Christ primarily perceived as male or human? What is the value of Jesus' humanity in human redemption? In light of the attitudes toward women and the physical in the early church, the answers will not be surprising. At the same time, if we are to understand the relationship between Christology and affirmative and negative attitudes toward women in the Christian church, we must consider them.

CHRIST, THE REDEEMER OF
ALL HUMANITY

Two major tendencies were at work in the development of Christology. One, which was in theory the dominant one, insisted on the unity of Christ's work as the redeemer of all. The other, which was influential in popular and devotional literature, centered more on Christ as the savior of humanity defined as normatively male. Although it is extremely difficult to separate these tendencies, I want to clarify the significance of these conflicting approaches.

Without question, the dominant theological assertion in Christian theology has been that there is one human race, and one redeemer, Jesus Christ. This assumption first emerges with accompanying theological rationale in the consideration of Christ as the Logos, illumining all human beings whom God has chosen (John 1:1–14). The Logos Christology was formulated by second-century Apologists who were the first Christians to self-consciously attempt to explain the Christian faith in the technical language of Greek philosophy of their era. It was based on an assumption of a unity in humanity derived from its common intellectual-rational nature. The one Logos, who became incarnate as Christ, created all human beings with a common spiritual nature according to his image. Because they share this common nature, all humanity is redeemed through the saving activity of the Logos.[9] This *soteriological* emphasis on the unity of humanity in redemption through the one Christ was a constant in major theological writings of the Christian tradition from the second century.[10]

During the christological debates of the first five centuries, none of the questions raised assumed anything other than a one Christ as the universal savior of males and females. At the Council of Chalcedon, where one might expect any hesitation about the proper designation for Christ to have been uttered, the formulation for designating Adam's being was "perfect in divinity, perfect in humanity." The council did not use the word for male, even though there was some precedent in the tradition for speaking of Christ as "God's man," male person.[11] The so-called Nicene Creed very plainly spoke of the incarnation as the son "becoming human," not "becoming a male person." The most common expression for human redemption was "Christ partook of our humanity, that we might participate in his divinity."[12]

Such an emphasis on the humanity of Christ and the equality of females and males is due to the focus on the human soul as determining who the person is. The body was secondary, except as the vehicle for the soul to exist in the world. When the necessity and even the goodness of the body was acknowledged and insisted on, that value of the body was never directly linked to anything which had to do with sexual differentiation. The soul was that part of the human which made us the image of God, and the body was good because it was the servant of the rational world.[13] Even when the ordination of women to the priesthood was prohibited, as in the *Constitutions of the Holy Apostles*, it was because Christians may not have priestesses as the pagans do (III,9). It was an *ad hominem* objection, not a theological one based on a distinct female body and nature.

Although the reality of the body in Christ and in redeemed human beings was firmly insisted on, they were very spiritualized and intellectual bodies. Furthermore, this realm of redemption was clearly placed in the hereafter, as far as the full consequences for human beings were concerned. In this life those bodies, as was Christ's, were subject to hunger, weakness, sexual urges, and all the weight of the material, animal disposition which hindered our sharing in the spiritual realm. Our present experience of bodies is negative or ambivalent, in this perspective. Theology also contained a strain of thought which placed great emphasis on humans as the link between the material and the spiritual, divine realm, but this was not the dominant opinion. Furthermore, even those who accepted this notion thought that passions were evil and disoriented humans from their proper role in the stewardship of creation.[14] The church, especially in the West, simply exhibited an inability to speak coherently of any redemption of the body in its concrete physical forms—as male and female in this life.[15]

THE ADAM/CHRIST DISTINCTION

The foregoing admission leads us to consider a second current in the development of Christian thought. On the one hand, one tradition insisted that we are all one in Christ, and that just as all sinned in Christ, so we are all made one in Christ (Gal. 3:38; Rom. 5:12–15; 1 Cor. 15:20–23, esp. 22, "For as in Adam all die, so also in Christ shall all be made alive."). If that tradition had dominated, women would have received explicit support for their equality with males through their redemption in Christ. But the Adam/Christ distinction found in Romans and 1 Corinthians could also be used to other purposes, because in the church, as in other societies, it turned out that some humans were more human than others. Because Adam and Christ were male persons, and the hierarchy in the church tended to be male-dominated, a periodically recurring theme among theologians, and even more frequently in popular art and devotional expressions, was that normative humanity was male humanity, and female humanity was just not quite as human.

For instance, in the thirteenth century, when Thomas Aquinas introduced Aristotelian metaphysics into Christian theological discourse, he accepted the decree of Aristotle's biology that women were inferior to males because they were misbegotten men. Because the body was the matter through which the mind experienced the world, women were inherently inferior to males, and their experience less adequate. Among other consequences, they were unsuitable for ordination. Because of their souls they could be baptized and saved, but by nature were not equal to males.

In the devotional literature of the early and medieval church, women were only admitted to spiritual equality with males through becoming like males in their spiritual lives, becoming virile in their virtues. The highest praise for a woman was that her virtue was as strong as a man's. At best, through giving up the exercise of their sexuality and remaining celibate, women could approximate the manly life of virtue, even though full equality in virtue would only be acknowledged in the next life, not in this one. After the Reformation, in Protestant circles, women were primarily exhorted to pursue virtues appropriate to their submissive female, and ordinarily married, state. Consequently their virtues were rather dull compared to male virtues, and were acclaimed as lower down the scale in the hierarchy of goodness than male virtues.

MALES AS NORMATIVE HUMANITY

Another major trend in the theological interpretation of human being which dominated devotional and artistic expression viewed Christ through anthropological glasses which considered males as normative humanity. The primal couple, Adam and Eve, who are redeemed by Christ, were split asunder in this interpretation, emphasizing the physical aspects of the first couple. Irenaeus, in the late second century, articulated this notion in his *Proof of the Apostolic Preaching,* in which he parallels Adam's creation from virgin soil and the will of God with Christ's incarnation in a virgin and the wisdom and will of God. Mary, who is the means through which Christ became incarnate, parallels Eve, who is the means through which Adam sinned.[16] Irenaeus does not say that Mary saves Eve, but his search for types drives a wedge between Eve and Adam, Christ and Mary, in their salvific activity.

I do not wish to comment on this notion as the origin of much Marian devotion, nor on the attitudes toward sexuality implicit in Irenaeus's assumptions. Minimally, one must conclude that this interpretation emphatically distinguishes the maleness of Jesus from the femaleness of Mary as central to redemption. Practically, its effect in devotion was to focus on Christ as the male savior. Because Christ was superior, just as Adam in his role as head of the human race was greater than Eve, the maleness of the savior was underscored. Because of other influences— the enduring influence of the mother goddess cults, the development of chivalry with its romantic attitudes toward women's compassion and love in the later middle ages—one can also understand the development of Mary as a countersavior, a female redeemer, almost in competition with her male son.

In light of the dominance of the two figures of Adam and Christ, was it any wonder that the *imago Dei* was imagined according to a male model, and Christ's maleness was underscored? The superior roles, God the Father, Christ the Redeemer, Adam the first head of humanity, were all male. The subordinates, Eve, Mary, holy Mother Church, and in a sense every soul in relationship to God, were female, that is, passive recipients of divine favor.[17] The resultant anthropology emphasized the dominance of the male, and popular devotion, supported by a patriarchal society, pictured and prayed to a male Christ. One of the unforeseen results was that during the course of the middle ages the male

Christ seemed so oppressive that increasingly people prayed to the Virgin Mary to intercede with her son to grant them mercy and salvation. Whatever the original intent of the split between male and female roles in the process of redemption, it actually encouraged a situation in which the male was either rejected in favor of the more accessible figure of the female, Mary, or in later devotion the figure of the Christ was feminized.

These images of Christ disclosed the varied effects of masculine domination in popular devotion to images of Christ. Despite various endeavors to reintegrate masculine and feminine images of the Christ, they were never quite successful in either the popular or theological realm, perhaps because those efforts always depended on certain stereotyped notions of masculine and feminine characteristics. Certainly the supposition of society that the female was inferior also influenced people. Another important factor in this development of Christology in the first few centuries is that dualisms and disjunctions were introduced in the very understanding of the divine and human in Christ.

THE ROAD TO CHALCEDON

Besides these various developments which directly affected the way the church connected Christ and maleness, another significant theological dispute was unfolding, not so often explored in relation to the church's attitude toward women. It centers around theological explanations of the relationship between the divine and the human in Jesus Christ. The five centuries of evolution and dispute in christological discussion from the time of Jesus until the Council of Chalcedon are extremely complicated.[18] The mainline Christian tradition asserts that Jesus was both divine and human, because only in this way could he have redeemed humanity. How is he both divine and human, and what does this reality mean to humanity?

For women the development was significant because the ideas which dominated the understanding of the Incarnation shaped a dualistic interpretation of Christ. The position which eventually dominated in the Latin church was used to justify a world-view in which the divine and human natures in Christ were separated, and a view of the human which denigrated humanity and especially the body permeated theology. This theological development did not cause the subordinate position of women. But in the particular constellation of factors in Western theological development, its dualism was quite damaging.

In response to some of the speculation of Arius of Alexandria, at the Council of Nicea in 325 the Christian community was pressured by Constantine, eager for speedy institutional unity, into accepting a formula which expressed Jesus Christ as being of the same reality as God. Athanasius and Arius's followers became leaders in a dispute about the meaning of this expression, and of the significance of the relationship of Christ to God and to humanity. Arius, anxious to protect the holiness of God, adopted a more conservative biblical interpretation. He asserted that Christ was not really divine, nor simply human, but an intermediary between the two. Athanasius countered Arian arguments by asserting that Christ was divine in the same way as was God the Father, and human as we are.[19]

Even though the Arian controversy in its original form was concluded in the institutional church of the Empire by the end of the fourth century through the theological work of the Cappadocian fathers and the political decisions made in support of the Nicean party, unsettled issues remained. Nestorius of Constantinople attempted to explain how Christ was divine and human by suggesting that the natures are quite separate and distinct, without mingling or confusion, linked through an act of personal willing.[20] Nestorius was not a very acute theologian, and he had the misfortune to be opposed by Cyril of Alexandria, who had a mind like a steel trap and, as bishop of Alexandria, resented the ecclesiastical influence and power of Constantinople. Cyril countered Nestorius by insisting that Christ's humanity and divinity were separate before the Incarnation, Christ the eternal Word existing timelessly in the Trinity, and in time assuming human nature. But after the moment of Incarnation, in the union the divine and human became one.[21] One of the interesting related aspects of this conflict was that Nestorius opposed the devotion of the monks and common people to Mary the Mother of God, insisting that she could be called the Mother of Christ, but not of God, because only the human nature of Christ could be said to have a mother. Cyril, on the other hand, asserted that because of the closeness of the union of the divine and human natures, Mary could indeed be called the Mother of God.

At the Council of Ephesus in 432, the right of the people to call Mary the Mother of God was upheld, but because the political and theological situation remained unsettled, it was not until the Council of Chalcedon in 453 that a formal declaration was promulgated. It asserted that Jesus Christ was fully divine in nature and fully human in nature, and that those natures were bound together in one person through the hypostatic union.[22] Nestorius was condemned, and Cyril's more extreme formulas were rejected. The whole development up to and including Chalcedon was extremely complex, but I would like to suggest two related and important points for the development of Western theology. (Orthodox theology was also adversely affected by it, but to assess the Orthodox attitudes toward women one has to take into account the unique social and cultural factors which shaped that theology and practice.) (1) Despite the language of reassurance used, Nestorius's interpretation, if not always his formulas, did in fact win the day at Chalcedon. (2) Nestorius's position encouraged dualism and a more negative view of human nature, which adversely affected the Western search for human wholeness.

Karekin Sarkissian, in *The Council of Chalcedon and the Armenian Church,* attempts to demonstrate the Armenian church's contention that the Council of Chalcedon represents in fact a triumph of Nestorianism, despite the rhetoric expended to deny it.[23] I do not intend here to recapitulate his arguments, which rest on close textual analysis, but I find them illuminating and at least in general convincing. The salient point for my argument is that Cyril was endeavoring in the context of his own anthropology and expressions about the human to express the close and unbreakable union between divine and human. In Cyril's theology and fifth-century "Monophysite" developments, the union rested on a very positive apprehension of the human being and its intrinsic capacity to know and be like God. Nestorius underlined the distinctions between divine and human because he did not perceive such a close relation between divine and human; consequently he insisted on the separation and the distinction between divine and human. Because he regarded them as so distinct by nature, his formulation about Christ had to keep a firm line of separation between the two.[24]

In the Latin West those formulations were particularly destructive because there was very little counterbalancing theology to insist on the closeness of divine and human. Consequently, the strict separation of divine and human was underscored. The theology of Augustine of Hippo, so important in the shaping of Latin theology, was permeated by a strong sense of the distance between God and sinful humanity. Especially important are his ideas about redemption and human participation in the divine life. Augustine had no theological argument to explain why the body as well as the spirit would be redeemed and share in eternal life. All he could do was insist that the body as well as the soul of the elect would be saved.[25]

The evolution in popular piety in the West is not best explained as the prevalence of a popular Monophysitism[26] but as the loss of Christ's humanity and the exclusive dominance of divinity. Periodic attempts to revive the focus on Christ's humanity as well as divinity emerged, but they ultimately issued in nineteenth-century liberal Protestantism's rejection of the divinity of Christ for humanity. A genuine union in the Incarnation between divine and human was seldom present in theology or devotion.

The anthropology behind the theology assumed that divine and human were radically different, and thus of course a union between the two was almost impossible to explain. The limit on the intrinsic possibilities of the human was very low. Put in the crassest possible terms, humanity was perceived in terms of immanence alone, and the divine in terms of transcendence. Sin was the fundamental characteristic of humanity *in concreto*. If one combines with this tendency the other suppositions we have considered, that woman was identified with the physical, and that males were perceived as normative humanity, woman's situation was indeed quite low. She was identifiable with the most unworthy and lowest aspects of a human nature that was already quite distinct from the divine. Men could console themselves that God's self-revelation came through male images, but women had not such comfort in most popular religion and even in most theological analyses. They were as far away from the divine as redeemable beings could be. Was there in classical Christianity, or could there ever be even now, any hope of a reconstruction of Christology which would be positively directed for women?

NOTES

1. A brief introduction to primary and secondary sources may be found in Richard A. Norris, *The Christological Controversy*, Sources of Early Christian Thought (Philadelphia: Fortress Press, 1980).

2. Judith Haupman, "Images of Women in the Talmud," in *Religion and Sexism*, ed. Rosemary Radford Ruether (New York: Simon & Schuster, 1974),

184–212. This work contains a good introduction concerning the ambivalent status of women in rabbinic Judaism.

3. Besides Leonard Swidler's *Biblical Affirmations of Women* (Philadelphia: Westminster Press, 1979), many studies of the role and status of women in the Scriptures have recently been published. Among these are: George Tavard, *Women in the Christian Tradition* (Notre Dame, Ind.: Univ. of Notre Dame Press, 1973), 36–47; Thierry Maertens, *The Advancing Dignity of Women in the Bible* (De Pere, Wisc.: St. Norbert Abbey Press, 1969); Karl Hermann Schelkle, *The Spirit and the Bride: Women in the Bible* (Collegeville, Minn.: Liturgical Press, 1980); John Otwell, *And Sarah Laughed: The Status of Women in the Old Testament* (Philadelphia: Westminster Press, 1976); Evelyn and Frank Stagg, *Women in the World of Jesus* (Philadelphia: Westminster Press, 1978); Werner Kelber, *Mark's Story of Jesus* (Philadelphia: Fortress Press, 1979); Bertil Gaetner, *Das Amt, der Mann, und die Frau im Neuen Testament* (Bad Windsheim: In Signo Crucis, 1960); Elisabeth Schüssler Fiorenza, "Women in the Pre-Pauline and Pauline Churches," *Union Seminary Quarterly Review* 33 (Spring and Summer 1978): 153–66; Elisabeth Schüssler Fiorenza, "Der Beitrag der Frau zur urchristlichen Geschichte," 60–91, and Luise Schottroff, "Frauen in Nachfolge Jesu in neutestamentlicher Zeit," 91–133, in *Traditionen der Befreiung: Sozialgeschichtliche Bibelauslegungen,* vol. 2 of *Frauen in der Bibel,* ed. Willy Schottroff and Wolfgang Stefemann (Munich: Chr. Kaiser, 1980).

4. Dorothy L. Sayers, *Are Women Human?,* ed. Mary Shideler (Grand Rapids: Wm. B. Eerdmans, 1971), 46–47.

5. Rosemary Radford Ruether, "Misogynism and Virginal Feminism in the Fathers of the Church," in *Religion and Sexism,* 150–83 and "Mothers of the Church: Ascetic Women in the Late Patristic Age," in *Women of Spirit,* ed. Rosemary Radford Ruether and Eleanor McLaughlin (New York: Simon & Schuster, 1979), 72–98.

6. Much more study needs to be done on women in early monasticism. For introductory primary material, see Palladius's *Lausiac History,* Ancient Christian Writers 34 (Westminster, Md.: Newman Press, 1964), esp. 89–90, 95–98, 117–19, 123–25, 134–38, 140–51.

7. In her article, "Misogynism and Virginal Feminism in the Fathers of the Church," Ruether identifies some of these strains of thought in patristic theology. Gregory of Nyssa's *On Virginity* exemplifies the more positive approach found among the Greek fathers. See Nicene and Post-Nicene Fathers, 2nd series (Grand Rapids: Wm. B. Eerdmans, 1976), V: 343–71. A study of the model of woman from this perspective is outlined in Patricia Wilson-Kastner's "Macrina: Virgin and Teacher," *Andrews University Seminary Studies* 17 (1979): 105–17.

8. Patricia Wilson-Kastner, in the preface to *A Lost Tradition: Women Writers of the Early Church,* P. Wilson-Kastner, G.R. Kastner et al. (Washing-

ton, D.C.: Univ. Press of America, 1981), vii–xxx, provides a general survey of the status of women in the early church. G.R. Kastner includes a brief introductory bibliography of Christian women writers and their milieu, pp. 173–78.

9. H.A. Wolfson, *The Philosophy of the Church Fathers* (Cambridge, Mass.: Harvard Univ. Press, 1970), 257–86; and *Religious Philosophy: A Group of Essays* (New York: Atheneum, 1965), 27–49.

10. J.N.D. Kelly, *Early Christian Doctrines* (New York: Harper & Row, 1960), 167–74. One has to be cautious in reading "man" or "men" in Kelly or in the translations of these early writers of the church. The original Greek is inclusive in the context of which Kelly writes, and usually means "human being" as such, not just males. The use of exclusive language in English scholarship often makes it difficult, especially for those who cannot read Greek, to be sure just what the early writer meant.

11. H. Denzinger and A. Schönmetzer, eds., *Enchiridion Symbolorum Definitionum Declarationem* (New York: Herder & Herder, 1966), 108.

12. For the Greek text of the Nicene Creed, see Denzinger-Schönmetzer, *Enchiridion,* 52. For a survey about the phrase "Christ partook of our humanity, that we might participate in his divinity," see Jules Gross, *La Divinization du Chrétien d'Après des Pères Grecs* (Paris: J. Gabalda, Librairie Lecoffre, 1938); W. Pesch, "Participation: Étude Biblique," 308–13, and H.R. Schlette, "Participation: Étude Historique et Étude d'Ensemble," 313–20, in *Encyclopédie de la Foi,* vol. 3, ed. H. Fries (Paris: Éditions du Cerf, 1966).

13. For instance, Gregory of Nyssa, *On Virginity,* 357–58.

14. D.S. Wallace-Hadrill, *The Greek Patristic View of Nature* (New York: Barnes & Noble, 1968), 40–79.

15. Good introductions to the theology of marriage may be found in: *The Encyclopedia of Theology,* s.v. "Marriage"; Derrick Sherwin Bailey, *The Mystery of Love and Marriage* (London: SCM Press, 1952); Roland H. Bainton, *What Christianity Says About Sex, Love, and Marriage* (New York: Association Press, 1957).

16. Irenaeus, *Proof of Apostolic Preaching,* Ancient Christian Writers 16 (Westminster, Md.: Newman Press, 1952), 68–69.

17. Marina Warner, *Alone of All Her Sex* (New York: Pocket Books, 1976), 50–67.

18. A basic account of theological developments may be found in Kelly's *Early Christian Doctrines,* 138–62, 223–51, 280–343.

19. Major primary sources in Norris, *Christological Controversy,* 83–102; Athanasius, *Select Works,* Nicene and Post-Nicene Fathers, 2nd series, vol. IV (Grand Rapids: Wm. B. Eerdmans, 1975); history of the developments of Arianism in Robert Gregg and Dennis Groh's *Early Arianism—A View of Salvation* (Philadelphia: Fortress Press, 1981); Thomas A. Kopecek, *A History of Neo-Arianism* (Philadelphia: Philadelphia Patristic Foundation, 1979).

20. Nestorius, *The Bazaar of Heracleides* (Oxford: At the Clarendon Press, 1925), 15–17.

21. Cyril of Alexandria, "Second Letter to Nestorius," in Norris, *Christological Controversy*, 135–40.

22. "Following therefore the holy Fathers, we all teach with one accord that the Lord Jesus Christ is one and the same, perfect in divinity and perfect in humanity, truly God and truly human, one from a reasonable soul and a body, consubstantial with the Father according to his divinity, and consubstantial with us according to his humanity. . . ." *Enchiridion Symbolorum*, 108 (author's translation).

23. Karekin Sarkissian, *The Council of Chalcedon and the Armenian Church* (New York: Armenian Church Prelacy, 1965) esp. 1–60, 174–218.

24. Alois Grillmeier and Heindrich Bacht, eds., *Das Konzil von Chalcedon*, 3 vols. (Wurzburg: Echter Verlag, 1951); Robert Sellers, *The Council of Chalcedon: A Historical-Doctrinal Survey* (London: SPCK, 1953).

25. Margaret R. Miles, *Augustine on the Body*, American Academy of Religion Dissertation Series (Missoula, Mont.: Scholars Press, 1979); Patricia Wilson-Kastner, "Note on the Iconoclastic Controversy: Greek and Latin Disagreements about Matter and Deification," *Andrews University Seminary Studies* 18 (Autumn 1980): 139–48.

26. Karl Rahner, "Current Problems in Christology," in *Theological Investigations* (Baltimore: Helicon Press, 1961), 1:159–60.

CHAPTER 5

Who Is This Christ?

DIVINE LOVE INCARNATE

"What, do you wish to know your Lord's meaning in this thing? Know it well: Love was his meaning. Who reveals it to you? Love. What did he reveal to you? Love. Why does he show it to you? For Love. Remain in this, and you will know more of the same. But you will never know different, without end. So I was taught that love is our Lord's meaning."[1] When the fourteenth-century anchorite Julian of Norwich wrote these words, she was expressing not only the meaning of the revelations given her, but also the significance of Christ for the Christian and for the whole world. For the Lady Julian love was not only the power that moved God to ensure that all things were created in love and that all would be well, and that in God we would find eternal life. Love was our beginning and end, the power and strength which holds all together in God. Love is the divine nature and life itself.[2]

In modern times Pierre Teilhard de Chardin spoke of love as the internal dynamic force within created beings which draws them to each other, and which ultimately explains the drawing together of the universe into an organic whole. The force of love, at work already in the most inert matter, is brought to its fruition in conscious personal relationship which draws the whole human race together in unity, that it may find its fulfillment in the God who is love.[3]

Love is not simply one factor among others in the dynamic of the universe itself and its relationship to God. It is the essence of the issue, the fundamental self-revelation of God, and the basic energy in which all holds together. If one is to understand who Jesus Christ is, to express the meaning of Christ in any context, then one's theological reconstruction must be focused on Christ as an expression of God's love. "In this the love of God was made manifest among us, that God sent his only

Son into the world, so that we might live through him" (1 John 4:9). In the process of exploring who Christ is and how the activity of God is made known to us through him, the meaning of love, as well as love as the meaning, begins to become clear to us.

The Christologies available in the mainline Christian tradition all appear to be riddled, tainted with strains of sexism, dualism, patriarchy, and a spirit which splits reality into separate components which have little real relationship to each other. Inevitably, the result is that women are identified with that which is inferior, and males are presented as the superior reality. Must all Christologies and Jesus Christ himself, therefore, be dismissed as hopelessly corrupted with an intrinsic sexism that is necessary to their very being? At this juncture a fundamental division of opinion occurs. It is not between those who are Christian and those who are not, but between those who believe that Jesus' male personhood is of the essence of his meaning as the Christ and those who do not. Some trivializations of Jesus that result from the former view have been well explored in the literature focusing on the questions of the ordination of women.[4] The most fundamental theological objection to such an approach is this: to identify Jesus with maleness (or Jewishness, or living in the first century, and so forth) is to miss the point of Jesus' significance and mission. Jesus became flesh so as to show forth the love of God among us, a love which is not merely an expression of good will, but the power of an energy which is the heart, core, and cohesive force of the universe. The Incarnation—the Word becoming flesh—shows us, as William Temple remarked, "God living a human life," that is, God manifest in a human life with all of the possibilities and limitations of human life.[5]

Within this context, Jesus' maleness, like the limited scope of his knowledge, his confinement to the first century in Palestine, and various other specifics of this life, are all examples of God's humility and self-emptying in living among us. Jesus the Christ is the expression of God in *a* human life, not *the* human life. To exalt the concrete details of Jesus' life in an exclusive way is to miss the whole point of the Incarnation, to misapprehend the nature of divine revelation, and in the most proper sense, to espouse heresy. It is the equivalent of mistaking the black type for the white page, or the spoken words for the gospel itself.

Consequently, what a reconstruction of Christology must do is look at the significance and meaning of Jesus Christ as a revelation of the divine love, in the process of learning more about Christ, humanity, and the divine love itself. The whole living tradition of the church through-out the ages must be reconsidered—the Scriptures, the writings of various theologians, liturgies, and popular beliefs and devotion. Some traditions, of course, are far more corrupted by sexism than others, but eventually all must be reexamined. Here we can only begin to make an overture for ways of integrating new insights and questions into the wealth of the Christian tradition. My conviction is that such a process is faithful to the fundamental insights of feminism as well as it is renewing and purifying for Christian theology.

The Christ whom we are considering is, after all, the living Christ, not simply a Palestinian rabbi of the first century. This Christ is the Incarnation of the eternal Word of God, in whom all things came to be, the center of the cosmos, who became human at a particular time and place to manifest God's love among us (John 1:1–18, Eph. 2:5–10, Col. 1:15–23). His presence continues among us, not only in the cosmos, but also very tangibly in the church which is called to be the meeting place for divine revelation and the self-awareness of humanity to God.

The search for the Jesus of history, as distinguished from the Christ of faith, which culminated in Albert Schweitzer's *Quest of the Historical Jesus* (1906), is consequently not one of ultimate importance for my theological position. Historical biblical studies are very helpful in understanding Jesus' life, teachings, and context. But finally, one must conclude that all of the biblical material offers different and developing perspectives on one Christ, incarnate in Jesus of Nazareth, who still lives in the cosmos and in the church. If one does not take this step, Christ is not one to be venerated, worshiped, or related to, but merely one whose impact can be studied in various guises or who may, under one or another interpretation, be inspiring as a model for behavior.[6]

In the exploration of the nature of Christ, some way must be found to express Christ as a revealer of God to humanity. Christ is the human expression of God to us, and thus we must try to understand what God meant in Christ. Christ is also the inclusive revelation of God's intention for humanity. In Christ we see something of how a divinely renewed humanity acts in the world. Christ is not simply the new male person, but one who shows all persons how to live. As a human he shows us what human self-possession and self-giving are. Thereby Christ shows us the link between divine and human, the cosmos and its conscious inhabitants. Only within such a context, with such concerns, can a feminist Christology emerge. Such a Christology will be feminist not in the sense of making Christ into a female, or merely attributing feminine characteristics to him, but in understanding the significance of Christ as embodying values and ideals which also are sought for and valued by feminists.

INTERPRETING CHRIST IN THE WORLD

Any endeavor to interpret the meaning of Jesus Christ for the world must focus on the ways in which, according to the New Testament and the theological tradition of the church, he reveals the divine in human terms for us: through his words and deeds.

Shubert Ogden underlined the significance of the theological interpretation of Jesus as the Christ (not merely the reconstruction of the historical person of Jesus) when he stated: "Everything depends on determining just who Jesus is . . . because he is the decisive re-presentation of the meaning of ultimate reality for us, and thus explicitly authorizes our authentic self-understanding as human beings."[7] If Christ is the one who tells us who God is to us, and who we ought to be to God, it is imperative to interpret this Christ adequately for the religious community. The focal points on which I have concentrated are Christ as the incarnate, crucified, and risen One. In the earliest preaching of the church and in its ancient creeds, those are the key aspects of the life of Jesus Christ, by which we understand who he is and who we are in him.

The Incarnate Word

In the prologue of John's Gospel (1:1–14), Jesus is introduced through what many contemporary Scripture scholars surmise to be an adaptation of an early Christian hymn. "In the beginning was the Word, and the Word was with God, and the Word was God. He was in the beginning with God; all things were made through him, and without him was not anything made that was made" (1:1–3).[8] This hymn continues a line of thought present in the Hebrew Bible, primarily in the later wisdom literature. Wisdom was the mind of God, increasingly personified as a female figure through whom God created the world. The hypostasis or personification of Wisdom in the intertestamental literature became a significant expression of the divine creative power and in the early writings of Philo of Alexandria (a contemporary of Jesus). Wisdom was frequently equated with the divine Logos, the intermediary in the divine creation of the world.[9] In the linguistic transformation from Hebrew to Greek, the feminine Hokmah (Wisdom) became identified with both the feminine Sophia and the masculine Logos. Joan Chamberlain Engelsman argues that because Jesus became identified with the Logos in the early Christian community, the masculine character of the Logos dominated and the feminine attributes of the divine surfaced in the figure of Mary.[10] In the Johannine literature, which became the focus through which the theologians of the early church read the wisdom literature of the Scriptures, the New Testament, Philo, and the platonic writings, Jesus is the incarnation of the eternal Logos. The Logos possesses the characteristics of Wisdom and the *shekinah* (the presence of God on earth), and in the Gospels partakes of attributes from both feminine and masculine personifications. In the New Testament the Logos is an ordering and creative force, the one from which all creation comes and in whom all have their being (John 1:1–5).

As the theology of the Logos developed in Christian theology, several dominant themes emerged.[11] The Logos is the eternally existing divine expression of the Father, the one through whom the world is created, and the one who becomes incarnate in Jesus Christ to heal and illumine all creation. Building on the Philonic notion of the Logos, from the time of the Apologists in the second century, theologians explained Jesus as the image of God, not just in the sense that all human beings are created in the image of God, but as the perfect image of divine wisdom and truth.

The Logos is the eternally existing expression of God, the mind of God which is God, equal to the God who is revealed as Father. In the fourth century Athanasius used the language of Logos to express the divinity of Christ:

> And again, Christ is the Word of God. . . . It remains then to say that he is from God Himself. . . . It is plain that the Word is not from nothing, not once was not, for he was ever; since he of whom he is the image, exists ever.[12]

As Athanasius and other theologians understood the Logos, it represented not simply a self-expression of God, but the perfect self-giving of God. God the Father gives himself to bring forth the Logos, the Word. Divine self-giving establishes a relationship of perfect equality and community between the Word and God.

God's self-giving in the Word not only produces the Word, but also is the expression for the activity of the Word toward the world. God the Father intends and empowers the creation, but it is through the Word that creation comes to be. We moderns think "Word" is something abstract and cerebral. Among the theologians of the early church who wrote about the Logos, it was far more specific: it was divine activity, a creative, expressive, and ordering force and one that created life. The divine Word retained many of those characteristics, which in the Hebrew Bible were attributed to Wisdom, of creativity and the understanding of all things. This creativity was sometimes personified in the female form. Clement of Alexandria, toward the end of the second century, was able to describe the breasts of Jesus the Word as ones which nourish creation.[13] The real significance did not lie in his use of specific feminine language, but in the fundamental notion of the creative Word as both including and transcending sexually linked personifications.

At the same time, however, the Logos imagery eventually focused on the comprehensiveness or inclusiveness of the Logos' creativity. For instance, the world was created through the eternal ideas in the mind of the Logos. The bond which was established between the Logos and the creation was not in fact merely conceptual, but involved a fundamental link between the Logos and creation. The very being of the world is an expression of the Logos, and all things come to be in existence through the sustaining and empowering love of the Logos, in whom all things live individually and as an organic whole (Col. 1:15–17). The Logos provides a link between God, the world, the human mind, and the human desire for understanding. Such contact was the result of a continuing relationship.

In the early church, a continuing line of development emerged: the Word was the sustaining source of the organic whole which is the world, the expression of divinity's creativity and self-manifestation in the world.[14] Because of the commitment of God in the self-giving activity of creation, the Word became incarnate to draw humanity, the conscious dimension of creation, to an ever fuller relation to the divine. In the second half of the second century Irenaeus, who introduced a most unfortunate theme into theology with the Adam/Christ, Eve/Mary comparison, articulated a far more positive position with his idea of recapitulation. The Incarnation, in his view, meant not merely that the Word took on a human life to repair the damage of sin, but that it was a necessary part of the maturation process of the human condition, to bring all things together in God.[15]

Medieval theologians such as St. Bonaventure in the thirteenth century intimated that the Incarnation is the most suitable expression of the relationship of the divine Word to creation. If human beings are created in the image of God, with a godlike spirit within them, invited by their very nature to experience a communion with God and relationship to others within that communion, that very Word who is the creator and who continuously upholds, nurtures, and sustains the creation *ought* to become incarnate. Such an incarnation of the Word would serve two purposes: to reveal the divine in human terms and to define the link between creation and the divine by explicitly including time and space in divine activity. Through the Word the relationship between God and the world, especially the conscious and reflexive part of the world— founded and set into motion in creation—is assumed into the divine life itself through the personal, indissoluble interconnectedness of the incarnate Christ.

Although the feminist theological community has debated the usefulness of Logos theology for a reconstruction of theology, it seems to me that it has a clear value. Christ as Logos draws our attention to the self-giving creativity of God, the eternal openness of God to the creation. The complex evolution of the world is not something that stands over against the divine; creativity is fundamental to the divine nature itself. God is not the same as creation, nor one part among other parts, but the fruitful source of the pluriformity of the visible world. The Word does not call creation into being in order to rule over a subservient reality forced to do deeds for God's benefits. The divine Word speaks in order that a reality—a potentiality—that is already contained within God may be brought to actuality.

The tradition of Wisdom in the Hebrew Bible certainly influenced the theology of the divine Word giving birth to creation as portrayed in the New Testament. Engelsman contends that the figure of the divine Word usurped the role of the feminine in the personification of the divine. One can also, I would suggest, judge this mixing of feminine and masculine elements in the Logos as positive because it permitted the introduction of feminine imagery in the portrayal of God active in the Logos. This style of expression could function as a way of overcoming exclusive sexual imagery by combining images attributed culturally to masculine and feminine into the single notion of divine creativity. Not only is the creative Word of God neither male nor female, but it also incorporates images of both identities and transcends both, as the Scriptures reveal.

One of the most compelling aspects of the Word is that it articulates divine creativity in all of its diversity, but centered through its unity in God. Multiplicity, diversity, and change are all characteristics contained in God's creativity, upholding and sustaining creaturely development and activity. The Word is the bearer of the complexity of creation, whose unity derives not from an artificial ordering or a static ideal, but through the dynamic of a love that centers the world—in all its diversity—in God. Due to their focus on God, the elements of creation are interdependent in one whole, and are capable of an infinite variety of interrelationships and shifting activities. The possibility for constant change, growth, diversity, and transformation exists because the Logos is the ever-fruitful womb of creation. The Word did not create by a one-time-only fiat, but constantly creates through an ever-active giving birth to creation, constantly sustains the ever-shifting currents of life in the cosmos.

Within this context of God's continuing creativity, the incarnation of the Word is an extension of that which God has been doing from the beginning. Julian of Norwich's image of Jesus our Mother is one way to express the Incarnation as the continuing birth-giving of the Word. One must acknowledge the limitations of human beings, bearing both matter and spirit within themselves, their freedom and ability to make choices, and their groping but ever-increasing sensitivity to the processes of the universe. In that light, it must also be said that the Incarnation affirms that all creation is good, that God is with creation, accepting its life into the divine life itself, while at the same time respecting the freedom and integrity of creation.

The Incarnation of the Word signals the goodness of all creation and God's continuing relationship to it in unambiguous acceptance. William Temple has remarked that Christianity is the most materialistic of all great religions,[16] and the Incarnation emphatically expresses this. In no other religion does God not only create matter but also accept it into the divine life itself, and remain in this living relationship for all eternity. Such an Incarnation was not merely an accident. Though thwarted by human sin, nevertheless it was God's intention to so incarnate divine creativity. Through the Incarnation, the multiplicity and diversity of God's creation is brought into the divine life. Through

Christ, the Incarnate One, the whole cosmos is drawn into a complete and free acceptance by God. Change and distinction are not destroyed or found to be illusory, but accepted and celebrated in their diversity, while finding unity through their centeredness in God revealed in Christ.

Redeeming Love

Even though one can (and even must) claim that creativity is an aspect of the divine reality, Scripture never explains why God created the world. Presumably, only God knows. Because neither the writer nor the reader of Scripture are divine, neither can say with certainty why God created the world. This question has proved to be a conundrum for philosophers and theologians throughout the ages. The best answer to the query seems to be that of Macrina, as reported by her brother Gregory of Nyssa. She replied that the question cannot be "settled by any efforts of the reasoning powers."[17] God never explains the creation; God made it. Any endeavor to discern God's motivation must be labeled second-guessing, an inference from what has been done, or hopeful speculation. But as the Scripture testifies, for motives which defy logical analysis, God loves the world; all of God's activities with and in the world relate to that love. To seek to know why God created is to enter into the mystery of the divine love.

When God made human beings, they were made free to nurture the creation in God's name, and free to respond to God and share in the divine goodness and love (Gen. 2:4—3:24). The freedom of God and of human beings on behalf of the whole creation is the basis for the relation of love which binds the world together with God: in God freedom and love are inextricably bound together. God's freedom is imaged in human freedom, the greatest gift which God gives to human beings, that in which they are most like God.[18]

In *The Trinity and the Kingdom,* Jürgen Moltmann most helpfully notes that freedom is not simply untrammeled choice; it involves rejoicing in the good.[19] Rather than accepting the classic form of the argument for that understanding of freedom, which depends on a particular interpretation of choice, the will, and good,[20] Moltmann refers us to the linguistic roots of freedom, the same as those for friendship. " '[F]ree' has the [same] etymological root as 'friendly'; its cognates in meaning are 'kind,' 'to be well-disposed,' 'to give pleasure.' "[21] The primary sense of "free" is beloved; the meaning comes from the term being applied to members of the household connected by ties of kinship to the head of the household, as distinguished from the status of slaves.[22]

To be free is to be a member of God's household, to be a child of God, responsible, loved, and loving, and to be united with others through the bonds of kinship and affection. For such freedom we humans were created, and through us, the whole world which we know. But even though God created us for such a destiny, God did not force humans to one or another response, and indeed could not so force them without destroying that which is at the core of our humanity, the capacity freely to accept and receive friendship, the sharing of the divine life. We do not find ourselves or our world so bonded. Instead we all may use our freedom to reject and to distort, as well as to love and receive. Who can imagine how the natural limitations and misfortunes that we experience are colored and shaped by our own incomprehensible twisting of our fundamental human freedom when we reject the purpose for which we were created?

Even the creation itself, which shares our fate because we are all bound into one, joins in the suffering which we bring upon ourselves: "For the creation waits with eager longing for the revealing of the children [RSV "sons"] of God; . . . because the creation itself will be set free from its bondage to decay and obtain the glorious liberty of the children of God" (Rom. 8:19, 21). The redemption we need, which the Scripture proclaims in Jesus Christ, constitutes not merely a forgiveness of personal evil or a deliverance from the body and the limits of creation, but a restoration of all creation. We are called to be stewards and priests in the community of friendship with God which has been promised from the beginning of humanity's existence.

In the incarnate One, Jesus Christ, who assumed our human condition, the creation is unified. But it must also be purified; evil as well as good is found in creation. How can the repudiation of the good, which we call evil, be transformed so that the cosmos may be whole and good? This process of transformation, which centers in Christ, culminates in the crucifixion.

Crucified Love

The figure of Jesus on the cross has been the subject of innumerable interpretations in theology, devotional literature, and the arts. But the Gospels themselves provide the key to all other interpretations. In the Gospel of John, in light of the events of Christ's life, death, and resurrection, the evangelist expresses the mystery of the divine self-giving on the cross. Volume after volume could be written about the crucifixion. One could explore the free self-giving of Jesus Christ in the crucifixion—the expression of the divine love for humanity.[23] I intend to focus first on the reconciling aspect of that crucifixion, exploring the notion of the cross as the unifier of alienation and painful diversity.

In the present world order diversity is usually experienced ambiguously. Because of the fragmentation, alienation, and division we experience in ourselves, others, and the world, that which is different, and opposite, whether within or without the self, appears to be threatening, opposed, and dangerous to us. Instead of allowing the multiplicity of creation to be celebrated as an expression of the riches of divine creativity, we experience and categorize the world as one in which various competing factors strive for dominance in a hostile world. When feminists speak of dualism, among other realities they mean this estrangement in which competition and control characterize the interrelationship of male-female, matter-spirit, intuition-reason, human-animal, and so forth.

In the crucifixion of Jesus Christ, freely undertaken and accepted, we see these dualisms adumbrated in one great action of reconciliation. The cross paradoxically transforms and reconciles all, even those realities which the present world perceives as opposed to each other.[24] John's Gospel locates this act of reconciliation in the figure of Jesus Christ on the cross, who in the humiliation of his passion is exalted as the Lord of all. "And I, when I am lifted up, will draw all people [RSV "men"] to myself" (John 12:32). John's whole account of Jesus' passion and death on the cross proclaims that this moment of humiliation is at the very same time the moment of supreme triumph—when the powerless one is all-conquering, the dead one gives life, the rejected one is the healer of all.[25] The radical abasement of God in Christ—in the crucifixion—is at that same instant the moment of exaltation and triumph.[26] Humiliation is glorification in the crucifixion, because Christ unites all in this one redemptive action (1 Cor. 1:22–25; Eph. 2:13–18; Rev. 5:6–10).

In this redemptive activity, the crucified Christ does not affirm that everything is caught up together in one undifferentiated whole in which diversity is ignored, and multiplicity erased. *In the cross* all that diversity, which is often a cause of division and alienation among humans, is embraced and unified in Christ. The crucifixion creates a dynamic whole through one human being's experience of the world's divisions and brokenness. And in one moment of time everything is unified as it had once been in the primordial harmony of creation.

In the fourth century, Gregory of Nyssa wrote about the cross in his *Great Catechism,* which was prepared for the use of those instructing catechumens:

> This is the very thing we learn from the Cross; it is divided into four parts, so that there are the projections, four in number from the central point where the whole converges upon itself; because he who at the hour of his pre-arranged death was stretched upon it binds together all things into himself, and by himself brings to one harmonious agreement the diverse natures of actual existences.[27]

The cross, according to the imagery used in the letter to the Ephesians, is the sign, the event, the moment, in which all the various alienated forces are reconciled and made one. Although twentieth-century Christians may have difficulties with Gregory's typology, and with his notion of Jesus' awareness of his own death, that does not affect the significance of what Gregory means. In the cross the cosmos is reunited; all those forces of alienation which have acted to dismember the universe are once again integrated in the cross, which encompasses the universe.

Because of the unity of divinity and humanity in the crucified Christ, the God who is self-giving and receiving accepts the fragmented human condition into the divine life for healing, and the humanity of Christ gathers into himself all the forces of alienation and destruction active in his own death. All the dualisms which divide, separate, cause pain, and support oppression and lack of communion with the other are all gathered together at the crucifixion, and Christ receives them. Because of who Christ is, redemption and healing are true not only for him individually but for the whole cosmos which he represents in himself as the new human being, the perfect priest. In the crucified one we behold a paradoxical union of those qualities which in life appear most unlike and incompatible: the absolutely conquered and the conquering ruler, the Suffering Servant and the enthroned Lord, the passive victim and the great high priest, the one who cannot save himself and the one in whom all creation finds its salvation. In the moment of the crucifixion Jesus Christ is all of these at one and the same time. Everything converges in him, and in his person and activity everything finds wholeness and meaning.

The crucifixion, therefore, witnesses to a truth feminism also affirms:

dualisms, be they of dominance and submission, male and female, matter and spirit, have no place in a Christian understanding of a redeemed universe. Any attempt to return to an alienated and fragmented world is to will the world back to the domain of sin, to give the world back to the demonic. Whatever configuration a world redeemed by the cross may assume, it can never allow itself to lapse back into a destructive schizophrenia. In the crucified one, in the very person of Jesus Christ, the alienation of the cosmos has been accepted and overcome.

Transforming Love

God's love in Christ transforms the cosmos as well as expressing in the crucifixion the love that unites the cosmos. Not only does the crucified incarnate one bind together all of the dividing forces of the world, but in Christ those demonic forces are transformed into a more God-focused existence (Eph. 1:20–23; Col. 1:15–17, 2:15). In the crucifixion Christ shows forth God's respect for human finite freedom in the most profound way, by accepting, respecting, and transforming it. Such freedom is freedom in the fullest sense, divine love expressed in self-giving and creativity, and human love in the acceptance of divine belovedness and the unforced return of this love to God and to others. In considering this kind of love, I want to explore two aspects of its power to transform: the first, the self-giving acceptance of humanity in its freedom; and the second, the transmutation of pain and suffering through the divine acceptance of negativity in the crucified Christ.

Nurturing Love

Periodically throughout the Christian tradition, the notion of Jesus our Mother emerges.[28] It represents an attempt to express the nurturing aspect of Christ's work among humanity—Jesus as a mother who seeks to find and heal all of her children. In the late Middle Ages Julian of Norwich developed this notion of Jesus our Mother to its highest theological sophistication. Her particular contribution included specifically connecting Jesus' motherhood with the crucifixion.

Over the course of at least twenty years Julian of Norwich developed her reflection about a vision of the crucified Christ which she had received, and it stands recorded in her book, *Showings*. Her meditations on the motherhood of Jesus are all derived from her fourteenth revelation, in which the crucified Christ appears as "the ground of prayer," the one through whom we have our contact with God and through whom God hears our supplications.[29] In this context, she apprehends Jesus as our Mother.

> Our substance is the higher part, which we have in our Father, God almighty; and the second person of the Trinity is our Mother in nature in our substantial creation, in whom we are founded and rooted, and he is the Mother of mercy in taking our sensuality. And so our Mother is working on us in various ways, in whom our parts are kept undivided; for in our Mother Christ we profit and increase, and in mercy he reforms and restores, and by the power of his passion, his death and his resurrection he unites us to his substance.[30]

She specifically links the motherhood of Jesus in the crucifixion with the creation: in creation human beings enter into the world, fall into sin, and are in need of a redeemer, and so the one in whom we are created becomes human to restore us to unity with God. Julian specifically links the crucifixion with child-bearing:

> O, what is that? But our true Mother Jesus, he alone bears us for joy and for endless life, blessed may he be. So he carries us within him in love and travail, until the full time when he wanted to suffer the sharpest thorns and cruel pains that ever were or will be, and at the last he died. And when he had finished, and had borne us so for bliss, still all this could not satisfy his wonderful love. And he revealed this in his great surpassing words of love: if I could suffer more, I would suffer more.[31]

The crucifixion is the moment of cosmic travail, when the creation that has been born—in love and in God—fully enters into the painful process of transformation. Julian draws on some of the prophetic images of God in labor to bring forth a renewed Israel and applies those notions to the crucifixion. The Christ who created is also the Christ who bears the agony of re-creation. By linking the creating and redeeming Christ, Julian balances any notion that the creative Word, the Christ, is detached from the creation, or that the creative activity of God is in our modern sense a rational or logical process. It is an act of love which involves pain, empathy, and concern. In entering into creative activity, Christ accepts all the pain involved, and would accept even more if the creation needed it for its rebirth in grace.

The form of Julian's visions of the crucified Christ and her insistence on the process of creation's entering into the bliss of friendship with God that will not be fulfilled in this life leads to the idea that God continuously gives birth to creation. The creation is still being reborn, human beings are still being brought forth from the womb of God, they are still being nurtured toward the completion of the process of birth. Through the sacraments (particularly Baptism and the Eucharist), which the medievals understood, following common patristic exegesis of John 19:34–37, as coming from the side of the crucified Christ, the crucified one continues to nourish his children to maturity.

> The mother can give her child suck of her milk, but our precious Mother Jesus, he can feed us with himself, and does it, most courteously and most tenderly, with the Blessed Sacrament, which is precious food of love life; . . . The mother may lay her child tenderly to her breast, but our tender Mother Jesus, he can lead us easily into his blessed breast, through his sweet open side, and show us there a part of the godhead and the joys of heaven, with inner certainty of endless bliss.[32]

The redemption offered to human beings in this process of earthly life, through the church and sacraments, is constantly given through the eternally crucified. His motherly love is constantly one of self-giving, always in labor, always in suffering until all are brought to eternal life, the full maturation of the children of God.

As she elaborates the metaphor of Jesus our Mother, and identifies the crucified one as the one who throughout all time bears us to eternal joy, Julian does not lose sight of the subjective human side of Jesus Christ's motherly role. The love to which humans are reborn cannot be automatically evoked, or coerced from them. Consequently, Julian spends much time exploring the way in which Jesus our Mother attracts us to the good, just as a loving Mother invites the child to maturity through the attractiveness of good, not the fear of punishment. Mother must help the child learn to walk, lure it to its first hesitating steps, being present to prevent it from hurting itself, but allowing it the painful freedom to totter and fall, and rise again. As the child grows older, it learns to be more mature through play and interaction with others. Mother puts the child with others, and watches them be disobedient, squabble, quarrel, hurt themselves, and exercise their own wrong preferences rather than Mother's right ones.

Jesus our Mother does not interfere in our becoming mature. Christ does not stop us from failing, falling, running away, and all the trials of growing up. We are free to make our own mistakes. But Jesus Christ our Mother is present to help us, to lift us up, to heal us if we are willing, if we desire to become mature, if we wish to become the children of God we are created to be. But the desire must come from within us.[33] Perhaps more graphically than any other of the medievals, Julian integrated human love and freedom, and the divine love and freedom, into the figure of the crucified Christ, our divine Mother.

One of the great values of this whole metaphor developed by Julian is that it underscores that language about Christ cannot properly be solely masculine, just as some of the Sophia language about the Word in the early church implied some feminine imagery. Julian's intentions are unmistakable. No one can pray to Jesus our Mother without being jarred into a recognition that the maleness of Jesus is quite accidental to his meaning as Christ. In the crucified one, masculine/feminine distinctions break down just as the language of male-Father, female-Mother falls into insignificance. In Jesus the dualities of sex stereotypes and roles are overcome in the perspective of the work of redemption.

More explicitly than any other imagery of the Christian tradition, the identification of Jesus as our Mother does affirm women's experience. Although one does not wish to fall into the trap of identifying women's experience with motherhood, or to substitute a female image of Christ for a male, the image of Christ as mother does incorporate an experience which biologically and psychologically concurs with women's experience. This is in and of itself a major contribution, which is still of value to theology today; there is no comparable scheme to Julian's. Her work and endeavors to incorporate the notion of divine motherhood into theology underline the truth that the woman's experience, just as the male experience, is an essential part of the expression of the divine relation to humanity, of the revealing act of God in the crucifixion of Christ.

Accepting the Rejection

On the cross, Jesus' last words in Matthew and Mark express pain, not simply the physical pain of torn muscles, suffocation, and the agonies of death, but also an expression of desolation, the depths of spiritual as well as physical pain. Jesus not only holds together in his person the cosmic forces of alienation and destruction, but he accepts them into his own person. He accepts his own rejection by the people he had come to redeem, and even by the Father who had sent him (Luke 23:34; Mark 16:34; Matt. 27:46).

Jesus came as a free expression of the divine love for the world. But

God's freedom also implies human freedom, operating in humanity's relationship to God. God invites humans to react to the divine initiative in love, to respond as the beloved ones of the household rather than as slaves whose responses are coerced. Such expectations involve risk, the danger of rejection.

Jesus Christ came into the human community to invite human responses, and some of those responses were of rejection. "He came to his own home, and his own people received him not" (John 1:11). Through Christ, God opens the divine life totally to this negativity, destruction, and rejection.

The perfect openness of divine love embraces human hatred and rejection. The pain which Jesus suffered was that of mockery and repudiation by those to whom he preached, betrayal in various guises, victimization by political, social, and religious systems which misused their rights and responsibilities, and death inflicted by those whom he loved, at the hands of those to whom he was well-disposed. His obedience unto death was not simply a passive response, but a divine acceptance of the worst the world could work, the martyrdom of a just person, and the repudiation of the servant of God, the denial of God's invitation.

But if Jesus' rejection by human beings was painful, even more wrenching was his sense of abandonment by God. One of the most shattering episodes in the Gospels is the end of Jesus' life, as reported in Matthew and Mark: the dying Jesus cries out with a loud voice, "My God, my God, why hast thou forsaken me?" and gives up his spirit (Matt. 27:45–50, Mark 15:33–37). No amount of explanation can take away the reality of the desolation expressed. Even though it is true that the final verses of Psalm 22, from which these words come, contain a triumphant hymn of praise to the God who delivers the psalmist from distress, those words are of hope for the future, not an alleviation of the present experience of desolation. He cries out in bitter complaint to God, and not even the glory of the resurrection to come can detract from the present reality of his aloneness, his separation from God.

Jürgen Moltmann continues the line of interpretation introduced by Luther: "He [Jesus] was assailed in his person, his very essence, in his relationship to the Father—in his divine sonship."[34] The very core of his person, his reason for being, the meaning of redemption, the community with the divine, creation's belonging to God: all was assaulted by this fundamental alienation. In the crucified one, God accepts into the divine life itself the possibility of alienation, rejection, pain, and the disintegration of the very self of God.

In Christ God accepts such alienation, powerful enough to dissolve the cosmos and destroy any hope of life, love, or community. But on the cross, at the same time that this most radical rejection by God is accepted, it is overcome. Christ expresses total abandonment and desolation, but never despair and hopelessness. Thus at the same time that one should not render the passion of Christ antiseptic and devoid of radical distress, one should not overlook that in the depths of his desolation words of hope are found. Jesus accepts rejection, he experiences it, but he never returns it. He does not "curse God, and die," as Job was urged to do by his wife. In his obedience he leaves open the hope that the silence of God, the sense of rejection he feels, the internal splitting of his being, is not final, but can be healed by the divine love which is the heart of the divine life itself. Even on the cross, his refusal to allow his own relationship to God, which he expressed in the language of father-son, to be dissolved by rejection proclaims his triumph over this alienation. In his refusal to reject his relation to God, even when the worst happens to him, he asserts a radical faith in the power of divine love that it will overcome evil and alienation even when there seems to be no hope in the cosmos, and the divine life itself is disrupted.

Certainly women have no monopoly over an absolutely accepting love, which is strong enough to deliver life from apparently hopeless and death-dealing situations. Nonetheless, one important role that has been accorded to women in most cultures is that of offering the strong and vulnerable love for others, which is expressed in child-bearing, making a home, serving others, accepting others even at the cost of personal pain. It would be demonic to say that such love should be characteristic of women alone, or that it is a peculiarly women's sort of love, just as it would be an expression of religious sadism to suggest that Jesus' desolation was in itself a good and pleasurable experience for him. Furthermore, such self-abandonment in love has been and continues to be an important aspect of the life that women lead. Rather than deny it or say that it is an aspect of women's lives to be rejected, it seems more constructive to celebrate the good which women are able to redeem out of impossible situations through the power of their steadfast love.

Such a recognition underlines the importance of strong and accepting love as a constructive force in human history, starkly revealing its power in the crucified one. This love is not an inferior, women's weak love, but the enduring love which maintains right relations in the cosmos when all other supports have failed. Such love is affirmed in Christ, the heart of the cosmos, the revelation of the love each of us is called to give to others and to the world, and also even to God. Women in particular have been models of a love which Christ shows us must be exercised by all humans as they work for the transformation of the world.

Reconciliation

In Christ the divine and human meet in a definitive way; therefore his life and death have an eternal divine significance. As the first followers of Jesus Christ insisted, his death on the cross was not simply one event among others in this life, but a time of reconciliation which remains meaningful, and through God's power is always present to us (1 Cor. 1:17–31). But the cross is not the final act of Jesus. In Christ God does not struggle with negativity and destruction on the cross forever; the tension of the paradox is resolved. In Christ's resurrection, alienation is overcome definitively in his person and the same healing and restoration is promised to the cosmos (Rom. 8:18–25).

In the early church (Acts 2:22–36, 4:33; 1 Cor. 15:12–22) the resurrection makes up the core of the Christian proclamation, the *sine qua non* of the faith of the disciples and the faith of the church. Indeed there are different stories of the resurrection with differing emphases and some diverse accounts of the events surrounding the raising of Jesus. Reginald Fuller has outlined the development of these various resurrection stories, and their kerygmatic and theological purpose, as well as their relation to the "historical events" of the resurrection.[35] The conclusions he reaches are essential for our endeavor. Through the proclamation of the resurrection, Fuller insists, the restoration and fulfillment of humanity through Jesus' dying and rising was proclaimed in the language of Jewish apocalyptic. Also proclaimed was the beginning of the fulfillment of Jesus' promise that "the reign of God is among you" in the life of the Spirit-filled community in which Jesus' early followers found that their lives were being transformed as Jesus' had been.[36]

If the end of Jesus' life simply occurred in his death on the cross, his promises to the disciples, the meaning of his message and his person to them would have been negated. The faith of the early church rested on encounters with the risen One, through whom their transformed lives were given to them.[37] As Fuller notes, the language in which this proclamation was clothed ranged from Jewish apocalyptic to the more Hellenistic kind. In this process of reflection on the meaning of the resurrection various dimensions of meaning were explored and identified in the Gospels and Epistles. Nonetheless, the primary meaning of the resurrection of Jesus always rests on the overcoming of the power of sin and death and the restoration of the world to its right relation of love and worship toward God.

In the risen Christ the fragmentation and alienation which are embraced in the crucifixion are reconciled in the raising from death of Christ. The fundamental significance of the resurrection to the Christian faith cannot be overestimated. In modern times Jürgen Moltmann, rephrasing Paul's claim in 1 Corinthians 15, has stated the case bluntly: "Christianity stands or falls with the reality of the raising of Jesus from the dead by God."[38] Various interpretations of the Christian gospel may focus on different dimensions of the resurrection, but the raising of Jesus is of the essence in any faith which lays claim to the name of Christian. The liturgies of the church extol this moment in almost incoherent ecstasy, as in the words of John of Damascus:

> Today the whole creation, heaven and earth and the deepest abysses of the earth are filled with joy. Let the whole universe celebrate the resurrection by which we are strengthened. . . . Yesterday I was buried with you, O Christ! Today I rise with you in your resurrection. Yesterday I was crucified with you: glorify me with you in your kingdom. Christ is risen from the dead! He has crushed death by his death and bestowed life upon those who lay in the tomb (Easter Canon of John of Damascus, 3rd Ode.).[39]

In the resurrection God gives us reconciliation in an absolute way, and promises that such reconciliation as we see in Christ is also for us, and not for us alone, but for the whole world which God has made. In 1 Corinthians 15 Paul outlines the logic of the resurrection faith. Christ is not raised as some proof of his pure teaching, or as a divine vindication of a just person unjustly executed. Paul notes that Christ Jesus has been raised as "the first fruits of those who have fallen asleep." His resurrection is an event and a promise: "so in Christ shall all be made alive." The resurrection is the declaration of the beginning of the end, the conquest of all that divided the world from God, and the definitive step in the process of cosmic reconciliation. For Paul, this process of transformation and reconciliation is definitive. Because of the resurrection the world has hope; it is assured that it has a future with God. The world's sure and certain hope is the promise of becoming one in God through Christ (esp. Rom. 5:15–21; 1 Cor. 15:42–58).

In the Pauline and Johannine tradition, the fundamental importance of the reality of the resurrection is underscored. The risen one is indeed a sign of God's love and restoration of humanity: the power of love to bring new life where death had appeared to triumph. The resurrection of Jesus Christ is, however, much more specific and precise than some general promise that flowers will bloom again from bomb-cratered fields. God acts in life specifically and in concrete cases, saving and restoring, not just supporting a vague powerful life force. In God nothing is lost, nothing falls through the cracks on the way to better times. Another living thing is not substituted for a living thing which has died or been crushed; life comes through God to that living thing which once was dead. All that is good, true, real, and created by God will have eternal life in God through the resurrection of Jesus.

Taking up the Pauline tradition, Gregory of Nyssa wrote of the "New Principle" at work in humanity through the resurrection. It is gradually being established in the human race through the divine life triumphant in Jesus' humanity, restoring human life to its true destiny and reuniting everything which is dissolving and alienated. The resurrection marks the beginning of the suffusing of humanity in the divine life and light. Because of its very creation, humanity is intended to share in God.[40] In his resurrection, as in the incarnation and crucifixion, Christ's significance is not simply that he is one isolated individual. He is *the* new human, the bearer in his own person of a humanity become what it truly should be, delivered from the seeds of its own destructiveness which it has nurtured and cherished. In Christ we are returned to God and ourselves, and begin the active process of returning to God in all areas of our lives.

Such a promise perceived in the resurrection rests on the confident affirmation of the unity of the human race, of our fundamental oneness despite those various factors which appear to divide us. If all of us are not human before God, the resurrection is an exercise in futility, or, at best, the beginning of redemption for males, Jews, rabbis, or whatever isolated category one perceives as defining the humanity of Jesus. Instead of affirming such division, the resurrection is the powerful sign of our unity. As Gregory of Nyssa notes, the principle of life in the resurrection of Jesus Christ is present "as though the whole of humanity was a single living being ... being imparted from the member [Christ] to the whole by virtue of the continuity and oneness of the nature."[41]

The Omega

In the book of Revelation, when the risen and glorified Christ speaks to John, he identifies himself as "the Alpha and the Omega, the beginning and the end" (Rev. 22:13), thus applying to himself the title used by God the Almighty in the beginning of Revelation (1:8). In modern times Teilhard de Chardin applied the term *Omega point* to "the divine center of convergence" toward which all is evolving.[42] He regards the Omega point as both the fulfillment of nature and the greatest gift of divine grace, at which point the entire developing world will find its fulfillment through entrance into the totality of Christ, which is both beyond all evolution and at the same time the fruit of it.

Teilhard de Chardin's vision is rooted not only in the terminology of Revelation but also in the Pauline and deutero-Pauline theology of the cosmic Christ.[43] In 1 Corinthians Paul speaks of all things being put under subjection to Christ, who will at the end be subjected to God, that God may be everything to everyone (1 Cor. 15:27–28). The eternal purpose of God, in Ephesians, is described as the "plan for the fulness of time, to unite all things in him, things in heaven and things on earth" (Eph. 1:10). This plan is fulfilled in the death, resurrection, and glorification of Christ by God, who "has put all things under his feet and has made him the head over all things for the church, which is his body, the fulness of him who fills all in all" (Eph. 1:19–23). Colossians presents a somewhat related notion of the fullness in Christ. The preexisting Christ is presented as the one in whom all was created, the first-born from the dead, in whom all the fullness of God dwells, and in whom all is reconciled. The mystery made known is that Christ is in us as the hope of glory, that we may become mature in him (Col. 1:15–29).

In the perspective of the reconciliation of evil and destructiveness through the resurrection, it is clear that the healing of the world is not simply an individual matter, but of importance to God as well as to us individuals. God from all eternity has intended creation to return the divine love in free responsiveness, and the death and resurrection of Christ are meaningful for the destiny of the cosmos. The universe is not merely the backdrop for the human drama; the whole universe is included in the cast. In Christ, through human healing, everything and everyone is being reconciled to God. The cosmos has meaning and purpose, not only in its individual parts but also in itself as a whole. The cosmos is a part of the divine fullness, which God has intended from the beginning, and which God is guiding to completion.

Such fulfillment, the Omega point, is not a dead monolithic entity. Because eternity describes the enduring character of the ever-living God, for the cosmos to enter more fully into the life of God means that it participates ever more fully in the ever-living God. Even though we cannot say with absolute certainty what God's life is (nor can we even define our own life with absolute precision), at the same time we can be certain that to enter into God's life does not mean to be absorbed into a static monad. We neither lose our own individuality, nor do we relinquish the growth, transformation, and development which are essential to the formation and maturing of relationships as we experience them. Life is movement, activity, and relationship, and however the cosmos may share in the divine life its participation must involve an active interrelationship with God.

Our entry into this relationship to God involves growth and continuing transformation, both on an individual and a cosmic scale. Because God is unbounded and ever-living, we never reach a point when we, or even all of us together as a universe, can claim to have exhausted the riches of the divine life. God's love and life are inexhaustible and unending, and thus our progress and growth in God is unending and we are capable of ever-increasing responsiveness to the divine love. Gregory of Nyssa even suggests that at the very heart of the divine purpose of creation was the intention that humanity should ever increase and change in its growth in the divine life.[44] An infinite growth into the divine image according to which we were created is the end for which we were made, and that for which the risen Christ frees us.

Such transformation and growth is not simply true of individual human beings, and of the whole human community; *it is true of all creation.* Christ is the firstborn of all creation, not just humanity. Humanity is a unity of all creation, the unification of the visible and invisible, the self-conscious organ of the awareness of and worship of God in the universe. Through the human priestly service, made possible because of the transforming resurrection of Christ, the whole cosmos is being brought to fulfillment in the fullness of God. Teilhard de Chardin expressed his understanding of that process:

I realize that the totality of all perfections, even natural perfections, is the necessary basis for that mystical and ultimate organism which you are constructing out of all things. You do not destroy, Lord, the beings you adopt for your building; but you transform them while preserving everything good that the centuries of creation have fashioned in them. The whole world is concentrated and uplifted in expectancy of union with the divine.[45]

Even though no one knows with absolute certitude what the words of Scripture in 1 Cor. 15:20–28 mean, or what Teilhard de Chardin or other interpreters intend, the ideas point to a profound understanding of God, Christ, and the destiny of the cosmos as a unity. No one knows where the Omega point of humanity, the unified world which has ended its visible cosmic evolution, is fulfilled, because no one has achieved that moment of time. Our only image is the one of the crucified and risen Christ through whom the fullness of all things comes—according to the promise of God that such a union will come.

The Process

In the risen and glorified Jesus, in anticipation, the cosmos is united in an infinite relationship of love with God. But what do we do in the meantime, while we await the consummation of our cosmic history? For us, this time of growth toward fulfillment with God is best spoken of as the time of life in the Spirit, a time that involves both waiting in the promise and living already in a developing reality of that eternal life with God. This time is the period of the church, the human community called by God to labor for the time when God will be everything to everyone (1 Cor. 15:28). It is a time for overcoming divisions and alienations, prejudices, hatred, and painful dualisms. The present is both a period of hopeful growth, as well as a bloodstained arena in which the forces of good labor toward their goal and sometimes painfully lose.

Through the Holy Spirit sent by the risen Christ the world is strengthened and renewed in its growth toward its fulfillment in God. In John's gospel, Jesus promises his disciples the Paraclete after he leaves them (John 16:7–11). In the events of Pentecost, recounted in the Acts of the Apostles, the ascension is presented as the completion of the resurrection, an affirmation of Jesus' glorification through his resurrection; and the coming of the Spirit at Pentecost is seen as the fulfillment of the promise made in the ascension. Until the Spirit comes, the disciples wait helplessly; after the coming of the Spirit the new age is proclaimed because the Spirit inspires them, strengthens them, teaches them what to do and how to spread the Gospel. The coming of the Spirit is the promise of the end-time (Acts of the Apostles 1—2).

Edward Schillebeeckx underscores the relationship between Easter and Pentecost. He notes the different connections between Easter and Pentecost in Luke and John, but stresses the common theme of the link between the resurrection and the coming of the Spirit. Only when Christ completes his human mission can the Spirit come[46] as the Spirit of Christ who strengthens and sustains the world while it "works out its salvation in fear and trembling."

The effect of the Spirit in the history of the biblical people is to create the church, the people who are called through the resurrection of Jesus to affirm the mighty acts of God in the crucifixion and resurrection, and the promises made to humanity and the cosmos through those events. To make such an assertion is not to claim that the Holy Spirit is only in the church, or that God is only present in and through the Christian community. It is blasphemous for any creature to prescribe limits for the divine activity. Even though I do not wish in this book to explore the nature of the interrelationships among various acts of God and responses to God outside the Judeo-Christian tradition, I would insist upon the reality and positive character of such relationships. Such connections among various communities of faith do not negate or deny the fundamental Christian claim that God is incarnate in Jesus Christ, and that the resurrection in Christ is efficacious for the whole cosmos. The church is the community in which God active in Christ is publicly acknowledged and adored, and through the power of the Spirit the church is at work in the world to bring it to its fulfillment.

Through Baptism in the name of the Father and the Son and the Holy Spirit persons enter into the church (Matt. 28:28). Through the active power of the Spirit the church is constantly being created and recreated as the communion of saints. Although the term "communion of saints" is not a biblical one, it expresses that notion one finds in passages such as 1 Corinthians 11—12, in which the Spirit, the church, the sacraments, and the community of believers are all explicitly interconnected. In the Spirit we are baptized, and in the Spirit we share in the Eucharist, the life of Christ among us. Through the Spirit we are made one community, with many individuals being given many gifts through the pleasure of the Spirit (1 Cor. 12:4–13). God has given all gifts in the Spirit, which are to be exercised to unify members of the community, just as a body is united to sustain one common life in which all benefit. For Paul the activity of the Spirit produces an organic unity. The Holy Spirit *is* a spirit of unity, giving life, sanctifying, that is, drawing all into the power of the love which unites all reality in God. Mutual respect and mutual service are the balancing factors through which the community retains its equilibrium as it moves toward the goal.

In Paul's theology the present reality of the church in and for the world is not without pain: "We know that the whole creation has been groaning in travail together until now; and not only the creation, but we ourselves, who have the first fruits of the Spirit, groan inwardly as we wait for adoption. . . . Likewise the Spirit helps us in our weakness" (Rom. 8:22–23; 26). The growth process is painful because the various forces of life and death are still in conflict, and we are all living in hope, waiting for each and every one of us—for our whole world—to grow into the fullness God offers us and to be gathered into the resurrection of Christ. In the meantime, as we grow toward fulfillment, we experience, observe, and inflict pain and evil, as well as good and positive development. Sometimes the pain is the fruit of sin, sometimes the necessary purging of the evil within and without. In all this travail the Spirit is with us in the promise of universal resurrection.

FEMINISM AND THE CHRIST

If in the cross of Christ we celebrate the power of sacrificial love, then in the resurrection we foresee triumph for all humanity, indeed for all the world, over the forces of alienation. One of the most fundamental insights of feminism is that the various divisions of hierarchy— alienation of humanity from the animate and inanimate world about it, dualisms of body and spirit—all need to be healed and overcome in us. In the resurrected Jesus, God has assured us that such healing has entered the world through the Spirit and is at work among us, and that this is the promise which God is fulfilling among us. The cosmic vision of feminism is not an illusory dream of naive individuals, but in its most thoroughgoing and radical form is the vision of the gospel, the promise made by God to the world through Jesus Christ. The struggles of feminism find their fullest context and their strongest promise of fulfillment in the risen Christ.

The resurrection of Christ is God's pledge to the divisions and dualisms in the world. Power and insignificance, matter and spirit, activity and inertia are united through the resurrection. The life of the risen Christ that pervades all things unites the divided, and continues as an active force for reconciliation in the world. Feminism, with its strong drive to both preserve the integrity of all beings and yet nurture the interconnectedness of the world, is confirmed in the figure of the risen Christ.

Such an ecological concern, which endeavors to conserve the world and its creatures, and yet also encourages the dynamism of life to surge through the cosmos, is manifest in the resurrection. The integrity of all reality is preserved, nurtured, and sustained. Such a dynamic growth process emerges from the creation itself. The resurrection does not signify an eternal imposition of meaning or purpose on the world; the resurrection is the fulfillment of the dynamic which is most profoundly within the world. The resurrection powerfully evokes and strengthens that which constitutes the most fundamental identity of the world, the urge which is at the heart of creation. Such respect for the evolution of life from this dynamic is at the heart of feminist concerns, often emerging in a rejection of what is perceived as the oppressive power of divine transcendence. In the resurrection such labeling of the power and love of God is shown to be a misunderstanding of both God and the way in which God acts in the world. In the resurrection the false dichotomies between transcendence and immanence are shown to be foreign to the God who is present in the risen Christ, who sustains and nurtures the world as an organic unity, respecting the integrity of the individual within the context of the dynamic of the whole.[47]

The incarnation, passion, resurrection of Christ, and the sending of the Spirit are not acts of an exclusive or oppressive God. No one can deny that Jesus the Christ was a male person, but the significance of the incarnation has to do with his humanity, not his maleness. When it was being true to its gospel the church understood this truth, although it has often been unfaithful indeed to its own faithful vision of Christ. In the crucifixion of Christ the dualisms and negativity that feminism seeks to overcome have been conquered. Through the resurrection the whole is healed and is being healed. Through the dynamic life of the risen Christ, the varied beings of the cosmos gather into one living whole in God, in which all that is good, beautiful, and true is nurtured and grows in the unending life of God. All reality, from the remotest subatomic particle to the most comprehensive and abstract idea, is living in God and being brought to its own completion as a part of God's gift of divine life to us. Any individual feminist may choose to reject this vision of Christ for any number of reasons. However, the figure of Christ remains our central symbol: one of inclusiveness, healing, and living unity, which fulfills the expectation of feminism.

If Christianity has not presented such an inclusive Christ to the world, the fault is not due to a fundamental exclusiveness or excuse for oppression and divisiveness found in Christ himself. Rather, the church's own lack of fidelity and vision has allowed it to be used by others, and itself to use Christ, as a sacred justification for social, political, economic, and religious repression. To acknowledge the reality of such evil done in Christ's name is to identify the negative effects of the human tendency to misuse freedom and to evoke the holy in the service of people's own selfish and oppressive end, rather than God's creative purpose.

NOTES

1. Julian of Norwich, *Showings,* ed. Edmund Colledge and James Walsh (New York: Paulist Press, 1978), 342.

2. Ibid., 191–92.

3. Pierre Teilhard de Chardin, *The Future of Man* (New York: Harper & Row, 1964), 98–100, 244–47.

4. See Paul K. Jewett, *The Ordination of Women* (Grand Rapids: Wm. B. Eerdmans, 1980), 35–46.

5. William Temple, *Christus Veritas* (London: Macmillan & Co., 1924), 139–42.

6. Various writers throughout the history of Christian thought have struggled with the uniqueness of the revelation of God in Christ. Besides the standard handbooks, see Alois Grillmeier, *Christ in Christian Tradition,* vol. 1 (Atlanta: John Knox Press, 1975); John Meyendorff, *Christ in Eastern Christian Thought* (Crestwood, N.Y.: St. Vladimir's Seminary Press, 1975). Here it should simply be noted that in the history of the Christian tradition there have been Christologies that insist on both the uniqueness of God's salvific revelation in Christ and the universal inclusiveness of the saving acts of God for the cosmos.

7. Shubert Ogden, *The Point of Christology* (San Francisco: Harper & Row, 1982), 82–83. Ogden and I would not agree about either who Jesus is or what Jesus means, but we are in accord about why it is important to form a Christology.

8. Wilbert F. Howard, "The Gospel According to St. John," in *The Interpreter's Bible* (Nashville: Abingdon Press, 1952) 8:463–64 and *The Interpreter's One Volume Commentary* (Nashville: Abingdon Press, 1971), 709–10; Raymond E. Brown, *The Gospel According to John I—XII,* Anchor Bible (Garden City, N.Y.: Doubleday & Co., 1966), 3–37, 519–24.

9. H.A. Wolfson, *Philo: Foundations of Religious Philosophy in Judaism, Christianity, and Islam* (Cambridge, Mass.: Harvard Univ. Press, 1947) 1:200–294; Joan Chamberlain Engelsman, *The Feminine Dimension of the Divine* (Philadelphia: Westminster Press, 1979), 74–120.

10. Engelsman, *Feminine Dimension of the Divine,* 98–120, esp. 114–19 for the Johannine portrait.

11. A history of this extremely complex theme may be found in G.L. Prestige, *God in Patristic Thought* (London: SPCK, 1952), 112–41; H.A. Wolfson, *Religious Philosophy: A Group of Essays* (New York: Atheneum, 1965), 27–37 and *The Philosophy of the Church Fathers: Faith, Trinity, Incarnation* (Cambridge, Mass.: Harvard Univ. Press, 1970), 1:177–286.

12. Athanasius, *Four Discourses Against the Arians,* Nicene and Post-Nicene Fathers, 2nd series (Grand Rapids: Wm. B. Eerdmans, 1975), IV:434.

13. Clement of Alexandria, *The Instructor,* Ante Nicene Fathers (Grand Rapids: Wm. B. Eerdmans, 1977), II: 296.

14. Esp. Paul Tillich, *Systematic Theology* (Chicago: Univ. of Chicago Press, 1967), 1:157–59; Ralph W. Inge, *The Platonic Tradition in English Religious Thought* (London: Longmans, Green & Co., 1926), 79–83.

15. Irenaeus, *Proof of the Apostolic Preaching,* Ancient Christian Writers 16 (Westminster, Md.: Newman Press, 1952), 1:51.

16. William Temple, *Readings in St. John's Gospel* (London: Macmillan & Co., 1959), xx.

17. Gregory of Nyssa, *On the Soul and the Resurrection,* Nicene and Post-Nicene Fathers, 2nd series (Grand Rapids: Wm. B. Eerdmans, 1976), V:457.

18. Gregory of Nyssa, *The Great Catechism,* Nicene and Post-Nicene Fathers, 2nd series, V:479.

19. Jürgen Moltmann, *The Trinity and the Kingdom: The Doctrine of God* (New York: Harper & Row, 1981), 55–56.

20. Thomas Aquinas, *Summa Theologica,* I, 83.

21. Moltmann, *Trinity and the Kingdom,* 56.

22. *Oxford English Dictionary,* s.v. "free."

23. Jürgen Moltmann, *The Crucified God: The Cross of Christ as the Foundation and Criticism of Christian Theology* (New York: Harper & Row, 1974).

24. The liturgies of the church are full of this language of paradox, especially during the feast of Easter and the days leading up to it. For instance, in the Byzantine liturgy for Great and Holy Saturday, the dirges of the burial of Christ

begin "O my Christ and my life, you were placed in a tomb . . ." and the second part: "O life bestowing Lord, it is right to magnify you,/for your hands were stretched out on the cross,/and in this way You destroyed the power of death." The Latin liturgy of Holy Saturday sings about the "night which enlightened the day . . . the night in which heavenly things are joined with earthly, divine with human." The medieval Easter sequence sings of the "leader of life, who has died, now reigns living." The language is poetic, transcending the normal laws of narrative or even of lyric. The breaking of the laws of language reflects the church's sense that the mystery of the passion of Christ breaks open reality in ways that force us to reassess and reinterpret all our accustomed understandings of the world and God's relationship to it. Such a paradoxical exploding of expected categories underlines the Christian assumption that redemption does not simply come from outside the world, but from the divine which lives and works from within to change, transform, expand, and fulfill all, at the same time it is in all and beyond all.

25. Rudolf Schnackenberg, *The Gospel According to St. John* (New York: Seabury Press, 1980), 2:398–410.

26. Nicholas of Cusa, *Unity and Reform: Selected Writings of Nicholas of Cusa* (Notre Dame, Ind.: Univ. of Notre Dame Press, 1962), 76.

27. Gregory of Nyssa, *The Great Catechism*, Nicene and Post-Nicene Fathers, 2nd series, V: 500.

28. André Cabbassut, "Une motion médiéval peu connue: la devotion à Jesus nôtre mère," *Revue d'Ascétique et de Mystique* 25 (1949): 234–45; Anselm of Canterbury, *The Prayers and Meditations of St. Anselm*, Eng. trans. S. Benedicta Wand (Harmondsworth, Eng.: Penguin Books, 1973), 153–56; Julian of Norwich, *Showings*, esp. intro., 85–97, text, 293–305.

29. Julian, *Showings*, 258–60.

30. Ibid., 294.

31. Ibid., 297–98.

32. Ibid., 298–99.

33. Ibid., 299–302.

34. Moltman, *Trinity and the Kingdom of God*, 77–80.

35. Reginald Fuller, *Formation of the Resurrection Narratives* (Philadelphia: Fortress Press, 1980).

36. Ibid., 168–69.

37. Ibid., 170–72.

38. Jürgen Moltmann, *Theology of Hope: On the Ground and the Implications for a Christian Eschatology* (New York: Harper & Row, 1969), 165.

39. *Byzantine Daily Worship* (Allendale, N.Y.: Alleluia Press, 1969), 849.

40. Gregory of Nyssa, *The Great Catechism*, 489–95.

41. Ibid., 499.

42. Teilhard de Chardin, *Future of Man*, 127.

43. Henri de Lubac, *The Religion of Teilhard de Chardin* (London: William Collins Sons, 1967), 173–84.

44. Gregory of Nyssa, *On the Soul and the Resurrection,* 453.

45. Teilhard de Chardin, from *Le Prêtre,* in *Hymn of the Universe* (New York: Harper & Row, 1965), 152.

46. Edward Schillebeeckx, *Christ: The Sacrament of the Encounter with God* (New York: Sheed and Ward, 1963), 34.

47. For an introduction to the historical and theological apprehensions and misapprehensions about the supernatural and transcendence, see Henri de Lubac, *The Mystery of the Supernatural* (New York: Herder & Herder, 1967).

CHAPTER 6

The Trinity

IMPORTANCE OF THE TRINITY

Within the Christian context, Jesus Christ is of fundamental significance to us because he shows us God's life and intentions toward us. At
the same time he also expresses the unity among humanity, its world
and the divine life. Jesus Christ's revelation of God is essential to us as
Christians because the God of Christianity is not a vaguely identified
divine power, but a trinitarian God, most commonly addressed as
Father, Son/Word, and Holy Spirit.[1]

At various times and in different ways the Christian notion of the
Trinity has been challenged; attacks became quite explicit after the
Reformation. Usually, the opponents of the doctrine of the Trinity
promised simultaneously a more biblical and a more rational understanding of God and of the whole way of approaching religion than that
given by the dominant Christian orthodoxy. In modern Christianity,
however, within the mainstream of the Christian tradition, we find
diverse understandings of the Trinity. Some would embrace it, but like
Friedrich Schleiermacher, regard the Trinity as being quite secondary to
the fundamental significance of Christianity. Others, such as Karl
Rahner, would acclaim the Trinity as being at the heart of the Christian
faith, but not a suitable mystery to be proclaimed as central to the
faithful. Others, like Jürgen Moltmann, would insist that not only is the
Trinity at the heart of Christian faith and worship but it also provides
the beginning point for the Christian interpretation of the world and
human social behavior.[2]

If one contends that the Trinity is at the heart of the Christian faith,
and if one asserts that an essential dimension of Christ's reality is that he
reveals God to humanity, then it would seem essential for Christians to
explore their notion of the God made known to them, the God whose

life they are invited to share. If Christians claim that this God is a trinitarian God, they must explore the Christian notion of the Trinity. Even if one claims that the Trinity is a mystery in the strictest sense, that is, by its very nature it cannot be completely understood by human beings, this means only that one must be appropriately cautious in making claims about what one knows about God. The mystery must still be explored.

The reason to explore Christianity's trinitarian deity stems from the centrality of God in the life and worship of the Christian, not simply in theological narrative. The Trinity is at the center of liturgical worship, even when explicit theological reflection is not taking place. To be baptized in the name of the Trinity, to hear a Scripture proclaimed which attests to a trinitarian God, and to partake of a Eucharist celebrated in the name of this Trinity is no mere accident or secondary matter; it is at the heart of faith. The Trinity is a core element of worship, which in turn becomes the lifeline for the transformation of the cosmos which the Christian professes is wrought through the divine love.[3]

For feminists the doctrine of the Trinity can be particularly important. I make such an assertion in spite of, rather than because of, the remarkable lack of enthusiasm for the Trinity in feminist circles. As a theological notion, the Trinity is more supportive of feminist values than is a strict monotheism. Popular monotheism is by far more of a support for patriarchy than trinitarianism, because the one God is always imaged as male. Despite the bitter disputes over trinitarian theology, the nineteenth- and twentieth-century endeavors to ignore the Trinity and focus on the unity of God, and more recent attempts to restore the Trinity to the center of theological efforts (Barth, Pannenberg, and Moltmann), nonetheless Western theology has tended to be overwhelmingly unitarian in its real theological considerations. Anyone reading more popular theological works with their discussions about God and Jesus Christ, with the Trinity added as a necessary if confusing traditional Christian addition, will find this confirmed.[4]

Such a development is unfortunate for those who regard the doctrine of the Trinity as vital to Christian theology, but it deprives feminist Christians of a particularly important, potentially inclusive notion of God. Put very simply, if one images God as three persons, it encourages one to focus on interrelationship as the core of divine reality, rather than on a single personal reality, almost always imaged as male. In monotheism God has historically been imaged as a male, patriarchal and dominating. The general Western Christian picturing of God, which sometimes appears even in theological explanation, has been to consider God as the one Father in heaven, who ruled all. Even when the Trinity was nominally acknowledged, the Father was the source, the dominant one, who begot the Son eternally, and the Spirit proceeded from them both. But the Father, who was creator, determined what would happen with creation, how biblical history would develop, how Jesus would redeem humankind, and what the Holy Spirit would do in the church. God the Father—like any father ought to be—was the head of the divine household. As the Christ was increasingly considered as human, and the Holy Spirit reduced to a ghostly whisper, God the Father was the only and unquestioned deity, modeling on a cosmic scale the male dominant behavior expected of all men, living in splendid and absolute isolation. Attached to such a deity, omnipotence, omniscience, absoluteness, and other usual attributes merely strengthened the patriarchal image of God. One could of course assert that God is not to be expressed in any sort of personal way, nor attribute any human characteristics to such a God; the divine is the power behind the cosmos, and that is all one may say. If one says this, of course, the position can be defended with integrity, but it is not Christian. An integrally Christian approach must deal with the biblical "Abba" of Jesus, the Word and Son of God, and the Spirit (Mark 14:36; John 1:1–14; Matt. 16:16; Acts 2:4; Matt. 28:19–20). One might substitute a unitarianism of the Mother Goddess for that of God the Father in heaven. Unhappily the same sorts of limitations are present as in the patriarchy, but with a woman's face.

The best option for feminists within a Christian context, I suggest, is offered by a trinitarian theology. One may offer a series of essentially negative and positive reasons for that assertion. Negatively, one may contend that the Trinity does not have to be so gender-specific as a more rigidly monotheistic picture of God. In the Christian tradition specific persons of the Trinity, usually the Holy Spirit, have been characterized in feminine language. Father and Son/Word usually are described in and addressed by male language. Sometimes, however, the Son is also called Mother, and the Spirit is spoken of as female. Although the linguistic history of the term "Holy Spirit" may influence this aspect of history, the nurturing role ascribed to the Spirit also bears on this old tradition.[5] In other words, even on the basis of its history, the doctrine permits inclusive language in its description of the deity. If one assumes that our imaging of the divine is intimately related to our notion of what human wholeness is, and humanity to the divine, then an expression of the divine which uses inclusive language by definition adds a helpful dimension to the discourse.

Furthermore, the notion of the Trinity is based on the self-revelation of a God who is at heart relational, not a bare unity, or an isolated divine monarch. A monarchical notion of the deity encourages the idea that relationship is secondary to God; a trinitarian concept asserts relationship as fundamental to the divine. Furthermore, to speak of the interrelationship of the persons of the Trinity as the key to understanding the divine is to establish personal interrelationship as the foundation of God's interaction with the world. A relational notion of God prevents us from imagining a unitary God creating in solitude and expecting a monolithic or uniform sort of response from a homogeneous creation. A trinitarian God at least accommodates the image of a deity who is far better compared to a family than the unmoved mover (if one is forced to choose between the two extremes), and who can be expected to create and invite this creation to respond creatively. The principle of coherence for the world which emerges from a trinitarian deity is not that of a divinely imposed fiat, but an affirmation of a diverse and interrelated creation.

WHAT IS THE TRINITY?

This history of the notion of the Trinity is a long and complex one. The question of the adequacy and suitability of this way of expressing the divine reality will continue to be discussed and explored within and without the Christian tradition. Here I would suggest that the doctrine of the Trinity can be a helpful and liberating means of expressing the divine reality for feminists in quest of the reality at the heart of the Christian faith.[6]

Modern historians of doctrine agree that the doctrine of the Trinity evolved from the early Christian efforts to explain the relationship—represented in the gospels—between Jesus and the God he came to reveal.[7] Of course, the doctrine represents an abstract formulation of Jesus' own expressions and other persons' reflections on their relationship with him and the effects it had. In spite of the complexities and formidable challenges, the maturation of the doctrine represented a necessary development, not only in the community's search for clarity about Jesus but also in its attempt to articulate the depth of its understanding about God. In its theological efforts, the searchers anchored their efforts in the worship life of Christianity in which Christians acclaimed God, Christ, and Holy Spirit as divine. The final formulation of the doctrine of the Trinity represented an effort to express this faith in language and thought rooted in the liturgical life of the early community, including its Hebrew Bible with its monotheistic faith, and with Hellenistic thought forms so familiar to educated Christians.

In the fourth century, the formula that came to dominate discussions about the Trinity was "three persons in one nature" (in Latin, "three persons in one substance or nature," in Greek, "three hypostases in one nature"). Various theologians wrote about what those terms meant; all equally insisted that these were the best possible terms which could be found, but that they were inadequate to express the divine reality.[8] The Trinity which Christians worship constitutes a relationship of three persons in one nature. The formulators of the classic language of the doctrine of the Trinity recognized relationship, interrelatedness, as central to God. We who are related to each other are united in the church with Jesus Christ, who tells us of his relationship with God. All Christian discourse and worship of the Trinity centers on relationship: among ourselves, the world, Christ, and God. The importance of relationship for theological anthropology is founded in the very nature of God, whose life of interrelationship we are invited to share through Christ.

"Relationship" is exceedingly complex, and many different metaphors, comparisons, and examples can be used to elucidate it. One can, as did Augustine and most Latin theologians following him, base one's comparisons with God's trinitarian life on internal personal relationships such as that between the person as thinking and as willing. One may also, as did Origen and the Greek theologians following him, write about relationship between persons as the best comparison for trinitarian life. The latter approach, referred to in modern times as the social theory of the Trinity, is not unknown to Western theology, and has been used by several recent theologians.[9]

"Relationship" is not simply something extrinsic to the person, an optional dimension to the person. Rather, to be a person is to be in relationship, to be a person because one is part of a social network. At this point the terms "relationship" and "person" used in trinitarian theology work together, and the descriptions of "person" and "relationship" are interrelated. In the third chapter, the human person was characterized as having two essential dimensions: one is the self-focused, the centered, the self-conscious; the other is the self-transcending, other-directed, outward-oriented part of the self. No person is or can be exclusively one or the other, although one or another dimension may be more or less well-developed. For the full person to develop, both a sense of self and self-transcendence in relationship are essential. In the development of the depths of the person, and not merely of isolated individual traits of the personality, the richness of self-transcendence and of self-centering nourish each other, and develop in dynamic tension. The more one reaches out to others and is accepting of connections, the more one comes into consciousness of and possession of the self.

If a person does not so develop, then either the psychic center of one's personal identity becomes so attenuated that there is no mature person reaching out, or the person becomes so self-absorbed that there is no growth or nurture from the environment and other selves, and the person withers and dries up. A person is one who is both self-possessed and self-giving, centered in the self yet at the same time transcending it. The divine Trinity which in Christ binds itself to the world is described in tradition as three persons in one nature; to use the term person indicates that God is a unity of three centers of awareness and centeredness who are also perfectly open and interdependent on each other.[10] The "persons" of the Trinity are three centers of divine identity, self-aware and self-giving in love, self-possessed yet freely transcending the self in eternal trinitarian interconnectedness.

Over the centuries the question of the unity of God has evoked considerable debate. Jürgen Moltmann has reasserted one venerable suggestion which would appear to have special value today. *Perichoresis* was a refinement by John of Damascus in the eighth century of the notion that each of the persons of the Trinity "not only subsists in the common divine substance; they also exist in their relations to the other Persons." John developed older theories about the relationship of the persons of the Trinity, asserting that the divine life takes place in God through the "exchange of energies" in the persons. "By virtue of their eternal love they live in one another to such an extent, and dwell in one another to such an extent, that they are one. It is a process of most perfect and intense empathy." The divine unity of the Trinity "lies in the eternal perichoresis of the Trinitarian persons."[11]

For Moltmann this unity is the heart of the Trinity; it is the divine substantial union based on love rather than lordship. Such an interpretation of trinitarian life not only provides an important opening for a reconsideration of the significance of the Trinity in Christian theology but also permits an understanding of the Trinity which is neither a patriarchal unitarianism nor polytheism. Furthermore, the notion is a valuable one for feminism. The notion of *perichoresis* implies the rich sharing of an unbounded love giving common life. Its linguistic origins identify a much more intense and lively interconnection than the roots of its medieval Latin equivalent (*circumincessio,* "sitting together"). This Greek word—*perichoresis*—signifies a dance round; and at the root of the theological term *perichoresis* is the image of dancing together.

Because feminism identifies interrelatedness and mutuality—equal, respectful, and nurturing relationships—as the basis of the world as it really is and as it ought to be, we can find no better understanding and image of the divine than that of the perfect and open relationships of love. In its divine dancing together, the Trinity of persons manifests the harmony and beauty of such a relationship; the unity of body, mind, movement, and sound in dance provide an engaging and comprehensive metaphor for the unity, comprehensiveness, and cooperative diversity in the divine life. As a metaphor, it is imperfect and ultimately breaks down if pushed too far. But for a feminist, the divine trinitarian dance is a far more appealing, inclusive, and revealing sign of the divine than the two seated white males and a dove, or a divine unity, male or female in image.[12] Such is the depth and commitment of the shared life of the Trinity that this eternal dance makes the three one: unfettered love creates a living stability stronger than an enforced bond through coercion or assertion of a preexisting divine substance of an ill-defined nature. As in a dance the diversity and the unity coexist; the unity of the dance is an active common life created by the dancers, whose very being as dancers is established through their full participation in the unity of the dance. In the universe the divine *perichoresis* summons everyone to join it in trinitarian eternal harmony.

According to such a vision of God the foundation of the divine life must be love. The love that is manifest in the incarnation, cross, and resurrection of Christ is expressed in the love of the Trinity. If one understands love as the self-communication or self-giving of the good, trinitarian life is perfect love. In perfect openness good gives unreservedly of itself (in traditional Christian language, the Father), and this love is a perfect receiving of love (the Son, or Word). Love self-giving and love receiving relate to each other in mutual harmony, and to love which is the perfect expression of this divine love (the Holy Spirit). As Moltmann notes, this self-expressiveness of the divine love supports the notion both of the self-communication of the divine love and also the preservation of those centers of divine life which for lack of a better term we call "persons."[13]

"God is eternally alive—eternally moving out into self-expression. He has the whole movement of absolute life in Himself," insists Charles Gore.[14] The Trinity is a perfect expression of divine love, according to Gore, because it so well focuses the living dynamism of the divine life of love. The trinitarian life is not a settled contractual arrangement, or a preprogrammed set of exercises, but a dynamic process of living communication.[15] God's own life is an ever-living communication in love; the self-expressiveness of good in God is an unending exchange, always in movement, because the divine life of love is constituted through such interchange and activity. The God whom Jesus made known was one who was a living God, and also a faithful God. A God whose very trinitarian unity is constituted through the eternal, incessant activity of love is the very divine nature absolutely living and absolutely true.

Although the divine Trinity is unbounded love, such love is not only expressed in perfect love to persons fully able to express it but also, for reasons unknown to us, to those who are able to give and receive in a variety of good and less good ways. Even though creation cannot, as we have noted, fully understand or appreciate God's life (or even its own life), through the being of Christ, God's trinitarian life is extended to creation, inviting it to share in the very divine love itself. That is, Christ came to heal, reconcile, and invite the world to enter freely and fully into the divine life.

By its very existence creation shows forth the divine goodness, but does not fully express it. It is as though one might have participants in the dance who were performing only one small movement but did not really know what they were doing, and did not perceive the beauty or significance of the dance. In Christ, human beings learn that each person, and the cosmos of which we are a part, is involved in a relationship with God. In the Trinity we have an invitation to enter fully and consciously into a relationship of love with each other and the world about us, within the overarching and undergirding exchange of love with the God who is the life of the dance, who is perfect harmony, peace, and love. In Christ, the Trinity becomes known to us and is active among us, and we are invited to share freely in the trinitarian life itself.

In Christ, in whom all things hold together (Col. 1:17), through whom God is incarnate among us, the trinitarian God calls us into the mystery of the free sharing of the divine life. Christian feminists acknowledge in this Christ the one who shows through his continued activity among us the trinitarian love which sustains us and invites us to an ever-increasing sharing of the divine life. Just as the trinitarian life is perfectly unforced and free, that is, constituted by the interconnectedness of love, so also God intends for the world. The dynamic of the cosmos with humanity in the cosmos and in relationship to each other emerges in uniting relations of love. This dynamism of love implies at the same time that the individuality of each creature is conserved and nourished. Such an apprehension of the divine life and of creation's sharing in the harmony of the divine life responds directly to the most fundamental questions of feminism about human life, its relation to the world, and the significance of the divine for humans seeking freedom.

TRINITY, WORLD, AND THE FUTURE

The trinitarian life into which Christ leads the world offers us insight into the way we ought to live, as well as a glimpse into the future God intends for our creation. Through the crucified and risen Christ we are introduced into a divine life which offers us a theological basis for constructing an ethics and for the transformation of society as it moves toward its cosmic fulfillment.

At first, the ambiguities and uncertainties, the fragmentation and perplexities of human life seem only tenuously related to a vision of reality which identifies harmony, interrelationships, and mutual love as its hallmark. But if one supposes that the dynamic of this complex and ever-changing world is directed toward healing the wounds caused by negativity and nurturing a diverse but united cosmos, then such a vision is the most helpful and fitting one possible for us. Thus we can say that trinitarian life gives life to the world, and the vision of the eternal trinitarian life shared with humanity and the world, transforming it, provides the world with the vision of itself and its future. Through God's unexacted invitation to the world to share in the divine life, God's future and the world's future become one.[16] Through the Incarnation, time, space, and the very notion of future become part of the divine reality. To perceive God as trinitarian, to pray to this trinitarian deity, to accept Christ as our link with this God, is also to accept ourselves as inextricably bound up in the divine life. The "end-time" does not simply provide me with a hope for my own personal fate, but promises God's reception of all of us and our movement toward God through the Christ "in whom all things hold together."

An ethics constructed with its perspective toward the world's future demands that above all we recognize that we and all our world are engaged in a process of growth, sometimes painful and sometimes pleasurable. In our very being we are called to share in God's life, and through Christ we are invited to participate in it more fully. In this eternal trinitarian life we are invited to live in the joy of the divine love which knows no bounds.

Growth and transformation are not matters which may be taken lightly; they are essentials of the Christian life. Furthermore, because of our participation in the divine life, our future with God is not simply individual and private, but corporate as well as personal. Our ethics must focus on ecological, social, and community issues within which specific personal questions, issues, and concerns find their proper place.

Such ethics impel us to share the divine life, which is the fundamental dynamic of the cosmos. Jürgen Moltmann has drawn some conclusions about characteristics of such ethics, and Mar Osthathios, from the Syrian Orthodox Church in South India, has tried to be more specific about the demands and possibilities of such ethics.[17] Although there will be differences of opinion and different perspectives and priorities because of varied cultural situations, certain values rooted in the trinitarian vision must emerge to shape human behavior, response, and actions. Through the incorporation of such values into the life of the world and its human community people can take part in the growth process—with its pains and pleasures—and hope for the future to which God invites us.

Although it requires a major effort just to outline the possible form of such an ethic, nevertheless certain approaches, values, and concerns can be identified. For me, three values seem to be crucial: inclusiveness, community, and freedom. Each of these is in dialogue with the other, and none is adequate alone. Together they provide a foundation for the reconstruction of human society which is integral to our sharing of the divine life.

Inclusiveness

To be inclusive is to value, gather, nurture, and find the significance of all that is good and true. By and large we humans are tribal, provincial, and selfish. Our horizons are acutely limited and we often fail to see and respect the good in the other; when we do we often try to quantify and to measure which is better and worse, gauging the other in terms of ourselves and our own ways of doing things. To be inclusive is to be open to the other, not to be bereft of judgment or discernment, but to decide to accept another person because of his or her worth, and to treasure other persons because of their contributions to the whole. There must be standards; judgments of good and evil must take place; but the basis for judging is our desire to include all that is positive, good, and true in perspective of the good which constitutes our cosmos. We act in faith that "the good" can be commonly identified. Such a desire to include is not on the periphery of our consciousness; it must be a central concern. We are called to seek, find, refine, and encourage the good. Such efforts are essential expressions of creative and redemptive love.

Community

To speak or write of community as a value would at first glance appear to be as meaningful as advocating that everyone be good. Very few would oppose such discourse. What one means by community and how one expects to move toward it are clear and necessary questions. Community comprehends the whole cosmos—animate, inanimate, animal, vegetable, mineral, human—with God. Community articulates unity and cooperation, interconnection on all levels, and yet it respects the integrity of the individual. Community signifies not just a sense of belonging, although such personal response should spring from being in a community. Community exists in and through the developing cohesiveness of the world only in imperfect and fragmented forms, but pointing us toward the increasing interconnectedness of the world.

Because community does not simply happen, but is being created through our cooperating energies, an adequate ethics moves us toward making choices that aid in building community. For instance, *class structures,* which categorize human beings because of their social standing through birth, denying basic rights and opportunities to some and awarding privilege to others, must be abolished through legislation, social reform, religious protest, and all available vehicles. *Sexism,* which denies the free development of the human person because of socially predetermined roles and expectations, must be expunged not only from people's minds and hearts, but also from the structures of society and from all expressions of the human and divine community. One could argue similarly about *racism,* which stratifies people into inferior and superior roles on the basis of skin color, and the many other repressive forces that inhibit our corporate development. The duty of Christians is not only to pray that such conditions not exist, but to act in accord with the prayer and aspiration, as well as the sense of the indwelling of the trinitarian God, in order to unify the fragmented world. Building community is a primary Christian task, with all its complexity and challenge.

Freedom

Freedom is a primary value because it is the inward animating power that creates community. Freedom, as Moltmann has suggested, indicates not simply the capacity to make choices, but the foundational relationships which enable one to choose.[18] To be free is to be animated by relationships of love toward the good. For any creature to be free, it must be capable of activities and responses which are rooted in relationships of love with God and with others. In such a relationship responsibility and self-directedness exist in a creative tension and balance in which the individual's development and the life of the community are encouraged and nurtured. Ideally, these are complementary principles; in our present experience conflict abounds between principles and the limited realities with which we live.

The ethical imperative of freedom urges us toward respect for the individual's capacity and responsibility to make choices from within, to develop according to her or his own sense of identity and needs. This sort of principle opposes the imposition of societal and legal strictures which artificially limit the development of a person. Margaret Fuller notes the damage done not only to individual women, especially blacks and native Americans, because of "arbitrary barriers," but also to the whole human community. When some are prevented from developing their potential, the whole community suffers because of our interconnectedness.[19] With awareness of the ambiguity of our human condition, yet with faith in its untapped good, a trinitarian ethics demands that the whole human community reorder itself to permit all human beings the maximum possibility to make their own decisions about how to develop themselves. Both freedom and responsibility spring from internal conviction. Necessary social reforms are fundamental because the person is both self-focused and self-transcending, and thus the social environment nurtures or stifles free development. Truly Christian ethics must be the midwife to renewing individuals and groups to bring forth community in the cosmos.

THE TRINITY: IMAGE AND LANGUAGE

If we understand Christ as the inclusive one who overcomes sexism and all other dualisms, how shall we speak of the Trinity? Does not trinitarian language itself focus on the exclusively masculine relationship—the Father, Son, and Holy Spirit? Even though the principles for reformation are present in the doctrine, is not the traditional language oppressive, and must it not be rejected? Such a question is of course significant for practical reasons raised by the liturgy and Christian education. Changing the accustomed language about God directly raises questions about the way in which members of the Christian community relate to their traditional roots, and the ease with which they may change that which has been handed down to them.

Fortunately, but also somewhat unhappily for some, the answers are quite complex. Part of the difficulty arises from the situation to which I pointed earlier: the Christian tradition offers a vast and more complex body of language and imagery about God than most of us recognize. The language of the mainline tradition has been dominantly, although not exclusively, male-oriented and as the rich and varied traditions are brought to our awareness again, a far richer language will be at our disposal.

To discard completely the Father-Son terminology of trinitarian language would present serious difficulties, because one could easily lose sight of the interpersonal aspects of the relationship. Intrinsically, Mother-Daughter images can be equally useful; ways could also be found to introduce and explore this expression of relationship. Terms such as "creator, redeemer, and sanctifier" can be helpful, but indicate only the relationship of God to us, rather than the inner life of the trinitarian God, in which we are invited to participate. The new formula may be a useful addition to liturgical and theological language, but it cannot be a substitute for the older formula.

At the heart of the matter is the way in which we use language to express our most basic feelings and understandings of the trinitarian God as our own awareness will permit us. Even to know the suggested rules for reform of theological language will not enable us to judge what we ought to do.[20] The key question seems to be what we wish to say about God and in what context we wish to say it. Such judgments involve not only rational considerations, but emotive ones as well. Language, as feminists are acutely aware, communicates affective dimensions as well as cognitive ones. Because of this phenomenon, inclusiveness in language about God does not mean that each word or phrase about the trinitarian God must be sex-neutral or have male and female (or exclusively female) terms side by side. Inclusiveness requires that old and new language be used in worship, teaching, and theological endeavors. Familiar language from Scripture and the tradition is a part of our identity, and truly conveys a part of the divine mystery to which it invites us. But unfamiliar phrases from the tradition (such as the womb of the Father, our Mother Jesus, and the Holy Spirit who gives us of her own life), as well as renewed biblical images and new expressions from contemporary experience, all belong to proper Christian theological and liturgical language. A delicate balance in the Christian community's self-expression now struggles to emerge between respecting people's limits in accepting and understanding less familiar language about God, and insuring that our language of theology, prayer, and education does become renewed and more inclusive. The pastoral needs and wants of those hesitant to change and those insistent on immediate renewal of our language about God must be respected. In practice this means much dialogue, common searching, willingness of each to hear the other, and openness to respect the integrity of the other while myself learning and being open to others' insights.

Above all, we are called to remember that our words about Christ and the Triune God are not simply religious memorials to feelings and past experiences. Our language expresses our relationship in a living cosmos with an ever-living God. The richer our expressions of relationship to this God, the more we as a community open ourselves to fuller communication with God. As our awareness of and openness to the manifold dimensions of God increase, we draw ourselves and our world closer to the divine mystery which made us and for which we are made.

NOTES

1. For brief treatments of the development of the Christian doctrine of the Trinity, see H.A. Wolfson, *Philosophy of the Fathers of the Church* (Cambridge, Mass.: Harvard Univ. Press, 1970), 141–363; G.L. Prestige, *God in Patristic Thought* (London: SPCK, 1952); Claude Welsh, *In This Name: The Doctrine of the Trinity in Contemporary Theology* (New York: Charles Scribner's Sons, 1972). Although certain other religious traditions, such as the Buddhist and the Hindu, have triune imagery and representations about the deity, they embody significant and fundamental differences from the Christian notion of the Trinity. See Ninian Smart, *World Religions: A Dialogue* (Baltimore: Penguin Books, 1960, 1966), 82–89.

2. Gordon Kaufman regards the Trinity as important for formal reasons, holding together the fullness of human experience of God, but not useful as a content for theology (*Systematic Theology: A Historicist Perspective* [New York: Charles Scribner's Sons, 1968], 243–52). Karl Rahner in *Encyclopedia of Theology: The Concise Sacramentum Mundi* (New York: Seabury Press, 1975), 303–8, cautions against too much emphasis on the immanent Trinity, in both theoretical and practical applications. Jürgen Moltmann, in *The Trinity and the Kingdom: The Doctrine of God* (New York: Harper & Row, 1981), 2–20, insists on the necessity of beginning with and remaining focused on the specifically Christian notion of the Trinity in one's dogmatic formulations. Robert W. Jenson, *The Triune Identity* (Philadelphia: Fortress Press, 1982), outlines a biblically based metaphysical interpretation which continues the work of the Cappadocians; his use of the more flexible theological base of Gregory and of Basil the Great, and his reliance on liturgies and the life of the church could be very helpful in further developments in feminist theology.

3. See Jürgen Moltmann, *The Trinity and the Kingdom,* 151–61; G. Wainwright, *Doxology: The Praise of God in Worship, Doctrine, and Life* (New York and London: Oxford Univ. Press, 1980), 15–117; Stephen Sykes, *The Integrity of Anglicanism* (London: Mowbrays, 1978), 98.

4. For examples of this tendency, consult *A New Catechism: Catholic Faith for Adults* (New York: Herder & Herder, 1967), 498–99; *The Common Catechism: A Book of Christian Faith,* ed. Johannes Feiner and Lukas Vischer (New York: Seabury Press, Crossroad Books, 1975), 229–31, 238–44.

5. For a brief review of this theme, see Leonard Swidler, *Biblical Affirmations of Women* (Philadelphia: Westminster Press, 1979), 21–73; Joan Chamberlain Engelsman, *The Feminine Dimension of the Divine* (Philadelphia: Westminster Press, 1979), 74–120, 152–53, and bibliography, 189–200. Kabbalistic literature discussing the feminine aspect of the divine is analyzed by Gershom Sholem, *Major Trends in Jewish Mysticism* (New York: Schocken Books, 1961), 205–43.

6. Letty Russell deals very little with the Trinity as such; Marjorie Suchocki, in an unpublished paper, "The Unmale God: Reconsidering the Trinity," attempts to reconstruct the doctrine from a process perspective to signify the "divine complexity-in-unity"; Jürgen Moltmann has made specific attempts to relate feminist concerns to his reconsideration of trinitarian theology in *Trinity and the Kingdom.* Of all these efforts, Moltmann's seems to me to offer the most fruitful possibilities. Robert Jenson, in *Triune Identity,* 13–16, 143–44, replies to accusations that the use of "Father" and "Son" in the liturgy and trinitarian theology is sexist. He asserts that use of these exclusive terms is not sexist because Jesus used these words and because use of "Father" breaks matriarchy in deity by abolishing the "whole attribution of sexuality to deity." To call God "Father" and "he" implies no superiority of masculine over feminine, Jenson contends. A fair criticism of his position requires far more than part of a footnote, but would begin by questioning his theory of language, which not only seems naive about the difficulties of translation (e.g., Aramaic to Greek to English), but also too rationalistic and unaware of language's metaphorical and symbolic dimensions. On these grounds one must deny his claims that exclusive language can ever be value-free, not exalting male above female, as well as his assumption that biblical language, even Jesus' own, need not be interpreted as fettered by its patriarchal context at the same time that it reveals the divine. Although Jenson knows that feminists criticize exclusively male language about God, he does not seem to understand their arguments or to take seriously the theological challenge.

7. J.N.D. Kelly, *Early Christian Doctrines* (New York: Harper & Row, 1960), 83–137, 252–79; Jaroslav Pelikan, *The Christian Tradition: A History of the Development of Doctrine,* vol. 1, *The Emergence of the Catholic Tradition (100–600)* (Chicago: Univ. of Chicago Press, 1971), 172–225.

8. For example, Boethius, "On the Trinity," in *Medieval Philosophy,* ed. H. Shapiro (New York: Random House, Modern Library, 1964), 72–83.

9. Welsh, *In This Name,* 259ff.; George Tavard, *The Vision of the Trinity* (Washington, D.C.: Univ. Press of America, 1981), 57–91.

10. Tavard, *Vision of the Trinity,* 84–86; Charles Gore, *The Reconstruction of Belief* (London: John Murray, 1926), 531–37, 548–49; Moltmann, *Trinity and the Kingdom,* 171–78.

11. Moltmann, *Trinity and the Kingdom,* 174–75.

12. A description of common medieval imagery for the Trinity as an old man with the crucified Jesus with a dove above is found in Frank Bottomley's *The Church Explorer's Guide* (London: Kaye and Ward, 1978), 144–45; in the Orthodox tradition, John Taylor, *Icon Painting* (New York: Mayflower Books, 1979), 51. Taylor also illustrates the three male travelers of Genesis 18 portrayed as the Trinity, p. 32.

13. Moltmann, *Trinity and the Kingdom,* 57.

14. Gore, *Reconstruction of Belief,* 548.

15. Some of the process theologians' reconstructions of the doctrine of the Trinity, such as Suchocki's "The Unmale God" and Norman Pittenger's *The Divine Trinity* (Philadelphia: United Church Press, 1977), esp. 114–18, have expounded the notion of the Trinity as an expression of God's activity toward the world. They have not attempted to deal with the Trinity as an expression of the inner life of God. James Spiceland in his "Process Theology," in *One God in Trinity,* ed. Peter Toon and James D. Spiceland (London: Samuel Bagster, 1980), 133–57, offers a critical appraisal of process theology and its relation to the notion of the Trinity.

16. Moltmann, *Trinity and the Kingdom,* 94–96. Carl E. Braaten, *The Future of God* (New York: Harper & Row, 1969), 102–8, presents a less speculative, more guarded, and biblically cautious version of this concept.

17. Moltmann, *Trinity and the Kingdom,* 191–222; Geervarghese Mar Osthathios, *Theology of a Classless Society* (London: Lutterworth Press, 1979).

18. Moltmann, *Trinity and the Kingdom,* 52–56.

19. Margaret Fuller, *Women in the Nineteenth Century* (New York: W.W. Norton Co., Norton Library, 1971), 37–38.

20. John B. Cobb, *Christ in a Pluralistic Age* (Philadelphia: Westminster Press, 1975), 258–264, has discussed the use of feminine imagery about the Trinity, affirming the need for new images of the Trinity and the inclusion of images from other religious traditions; Moltmann, in *Trinity and the Kingdom,* 57, 164–65, focuses on the breaking down of gender-identified roles and images in the activity of and language about the trinitarian God. Significant work has been done in recent years to provide educational and liturgical resources in nonsexist language. See, for example, Marianne Sawicki, *Faith and Sexism: Guidelines for Religious Educators* (New York: Seabury Press, 1979), 19–38, *All May Be One.* A Guide to Inclusive Church Language Task Force on Women, Presbytery of the Twin Cities Area (Minneapolis: Presbytery of the Twin Cities Area, 1979), 19–21; and *Worship: Inclusive Language Resources,* Office for Church Life and Leadership, United Church of Christ (St. Louis: Office for Church Life and Leadership, 1977), 1–4. See also other resources such as *Guidelines for Avoiding Bias for Writers and Editors* (New York: Office for Communications, Lutheran Church in America).

Epilogue

Over a year has passed since I began to write this work in its present form. Developments in feminist scholarship continue to support my opinion that this book is a partial contribution to a dialogue which has just begun. The contemporary feminist movement is exceedingly diverse and continues to evolve. Because Christianity is also a highly complex phenomenon, its relationship to feminism within and without itself is in constant flux. My essay in Christology identifies participants in the discussion, suggests some lines of development, and raises far more questions than those to which it responds.

Today women scholars, theologians, and pastors continue the quest to be feminists and Christians with integrity. At the same time they reclaim women's roots from the past, they face contemporary psychological, social, and intellectual needs of women as they try to imagine a world purged of its sexist prejudices and oppressions. Practical issues abound as the faltering economy underlines the second-class status of women in society. As women professionals in the church compete with males and with other women for decreasing numbers of positions, they are tempted to accept the status quo, if only the church will admit them into its structures. Challenging questions about practice and theory are forgotten or suppressed as women try to adapt.

Such pressures encourage women to ignore the wide-ranging and potentially convention-shattering work that they ought to be doing in history, scriptural studies, theology, and ethics. When survival becomes their central concern, the great temptation for most women, no matter how great their feminist convictions, is to abandon renewal of corporate life and focus on individual psychic and economic survival.

In seminaries and universities, and nontraditional centers of Christian feminist reflection, an ahistorical perspective is frequently espoused. Whether through creation of an imaginary past or by identifying feminism exclusively with one or another contemporary system of thought, feminists ignore or deny the past and any value it might have for the present or future. The illusory attempt to pretend that Christian feminist positions can be created from nothing, or can spring fully formed from the air, remains compelling for contemporary Americans.

My efforts in this book underscore, I hope, my firm conviction that a far more difficult and comprehensive effort lies ahead of us. My work is a minor essay; others are presently engaged in and must continue to labor in the wide-ranging, demanding, yet rewarding effort to rethink, reimagine, and reconstruct Christianity from the perspective of a feminism faithful to God's self-expression and self-giving in Christ. Both a new method and an extensive agenda are demanded of such pioneers.

A method for this quest involves, as I have tried to demonstrate, an identification of feminist values and insights and an appreciation of the feminist criticisms of Christianity. At the same time this method asks how God is revealed and humanity interpreted in the goodness of Christianity. Such an effort demands a return to the sources, to ask not only what has been said theologically, but why it was said and what it meant. Such an inquiry uncovers a richness in the self-revelation of God in Christ that discloses more inclusiveness than Christianity has often in fact dared to preach. We can uncover much from the past which already informs the present, helping us relate to the roots and sources of our lives, and directing us toward an immeasurably richer future.

I have sketched some ideas about a reconstruction of Christology and the doctrine of the Trinity; much more can be done, from my own and from other perspectives, about these two issues. The Christian notion of the Holy Spirit is one rich with possibilities, and has the historical advantage of often being the focus for the attribution of feminine characteristics, imagery, and language to God. Ecclesiology—with its mixed messages to women, at once exalting "Mother Church" and yet stressing the subordination of all humanity, especially of women, to the divine—must be reconsidered and reworked. Theological anthropology, which I only briefly attended to, must be comprehensively reconstructed to explore individual and corporate equality, yet allow for individual capabilities. Liturgical study, the theology of prayer, and ethics have inadequately allowed women their humanity in the past, and must be reformed to express a renewed vision about God and humanity. All of these disciplines must also expand their scope to include not only God and humanity, but the whole cosmos which comes from God and of which humanity is only one part.

Such an effort will cost many persons many lifetimes of reflection and practice, yet the labor is essential to the birth of the world that feminism seeks. I have begun with Christology because for the Christian it holds the key for the direction in which all further developments will take place. My attempt underlines, I trust, that if there is any hope for our world at all, it is based on a vision of the cosmos as an interconnected whole, founded in and related to God. In this way of theologizing, Christ provides the interpretive key to this interrelatedness, because Christ is the way in which God relates to the world, and we and our cosmos relate to God. This book should serve as one more signpost along the way: in the Christ "all things hold together" as we grow toward that fulfillment of our world in which "God may be everything to everyone."

Index of Names

Anselm of Canterbury, 118 n.28
Aristotle, 45, 46
Arius, 82
Athanasius, 82, 93, 117 n.12
Augustine of Hippo, 30, 46, 63, 83, 84

Bach, Heindrich, 87 n.24
Bailey, Derrick Sherwin, 86 n.15
Bainton, Roland, 86 n.15
Barbour, Ian, 53 n.6
Barth, Karl, 122
Bergson, Henri, 46
Boetheius, 136 n.8
Bonaventure, 95
Bottomley, Frank, 136 n.12
Braaten, Carl, 137 n.16
Brock, Rita, 29–30, 37 nn.57–59, 61–62
Bronowski, Jacob, 53 n.6
Brown, Raymond E., 117 n.8
Burns, James Edgar, 38 n.78
Bruce, Michael, 9 n.5

Cabbassut, André, 118 n.28
Capon, Robert, 68 n.8
Chalcedon, Council of, 78, 81, 83, 86 n.11, 87 n.22
Christ, Carol, 1, 8 n.2, 13–14, 19, 21, 22, 35 nn.5–7, 36 nn.19, 22, 28, 29
Clement of Alexandria, 31, 94, 117 n.13
Cobb, John, 137 n.20
Constitutions of the Holy Apostles, 78

Cooper, Burton, 30–31, 37 nn.63–65
Cyril of Alexandria, 82, 83, 87 n.21, 117 n.13

Daly, Mary, 1, 8 n.1, 12–13, 23, 28–29, 30, 35 nn.1–4, 37 nn.50–51, n.53, 50
Deloria, Vine, 40, 52 n.3
Derrida, Jacques, 17
Descartes, Rene, 41, 46
Dewey, Margaret, 20, 36 n.21
Dickie, George, 10 n.11
Dowell, Susan, 9 n.7
Duffield, G. E., 9 n.5

Edwards, Jonathan, 59, 68 n.6
Engelsman, Joan Chamberlain, 4, 9 nn.7, 10, 24–25, 31, 36 n.39, 37 nn.66–67, 93, 117 nn.9, 10, 135 n.5
Ephesus, Council of, 82

Feiner, Johannes, 135 n.4
Fiorenza, Elizabeth Schüssler, 85 n.3
Fletcher, Joseph, 68 n.9
Foh, Susan T., 8 n.3
Ford, Lewis, 37 n.60
Freud, Sigmund, 22
Fuller, Margaret, 54 n.11, 66, 137 n.19
Fuller, Reginald, 107–8, 118 nn.35–37

Gaetner, Bertil, 85 n.3
Gamov, George, 53 n.6
Gilligan, Carol, 68 n.10

Goldenberg, Naomi, 1, 4, 9 n.9,
    21–22, 28, 36 nn. 24–27, 37 n. 49
Gore, Charles, 128, 136 n. 10, 137
    n. 14
Gregg, Robert, 86 n. 19
Gregory of Nyssa, 58, 59, 67 n. 4, 68
    n. 5, 86 n. 13, 97, 100, 109–11, 117
    nn. 17, 18, 118 nn. 27, 40–41, 119
    n. 44
Gribbon, John, 53 n. 6
Grillmeier, Alois, 87 n. 24, 116 n. 6
Groh, Dennis, 86 n. 19
Gross, Jules, 86 n. 12
Gutierrez, Gustavo, 69 n. 5

Haag, Herbert, 68 n. 13
Hamilton, Peter, 53 n. 7
Harkness, Georgia, 36 n. 37
Hartshorne, Charles, 53 n. 7
Haupman, Judith, 84 n. 2
Heilbrun, Carol, 16–17, 35 nn.
    14–15
Hewitt, Emily, 9 n. 5
Heyward, Carter, 26–27, 28, 37
    nn. 45–47
Hiatt, Susanne R., 9 n. 5
Howard, Wilbert F., 117 n. 8
Hurcombe, Linda, 9 n. 7

Inge, Ralph W., 117 n. 14
Irenaeus, 80, 86 n. 16, 94–95, 117
    n. 15

Jenson, Robert W., 135 n. 2, 136 n. 6
Jewett, Paul K., 9 n. 5, 67 n. 3, 116 n. 4
John of Damascus, 108, 126
John Paul II, 9 n. 5

Kant, Immanuel, 41, 42
Kastner, G. R., 86 n. 8
Kaufmann, Gordon, 135 n. 2
Kelber, Werner, 85 n. 3
Kelly, J. N. D., 86 nn. 10, 18, 136 n. 6
Kopacek, Thomas A., 86 n. 19

Lacan, Jacques, 17

Lantero, Emily Huntress, 9 n. 7
Lavin, Roger, 67 n. 2
Leakey, Richard, 67 n. 2
Levy, Donald, 68 n. 2
Lonergan, Bernard, 39, 46, 52 nn. 1,
    4, 54 n. 12
Lubac, Henri de, 53 n. 7, 119 nn. 43,
    47

Macrina, 97
Maertens, Thierry, 85 n. 3
Mascall, Eric L., 8 n. 4
McFague, Sally, 4
McLaughlin, Eleanor, 3, 9 n. 6, 24, 36
    n. 38
Mead, Margaret, 68 n. 10
Menninger, Karl, 69 n. 14
Merchant, Carolyn, 42, 52 n. 5
Meyendorff, John, 116 n. 6
Micks, Marianne, 4, 9 n. 7, 67 n. 2
Miles, Margaret, 87 n. 25
Miller, Casey, 67 n. 1
Moltmann, Jürgen, 97–98, 105–6,
    117 nn. 19, 21, 23, 118 nn. 34, 38,
    121, 126–27, 130, 132, 135 nn. 2,
    3, 136 nn. 6, 10, 11, 13, 137
    nn. 16–18
Morris, Joan, 3, 9 n. 6

Nelson, James, 53 n. 8
Nestorius, 82–83, 87 n. 20
Newton, Isaac, 42
Nicholas of Cusa, 118 n. 26
Nogar, Raymond, 54, n. 10
Norris, Richard A., 84 n. 1, 86 n. 19

Ochs, Carol, 27–28, 36 n. 48
Ogden, Shubert, 92, 116 n. 7
Osthathios, Geervarghese Mar, 130,
    137 n. 17
Otwell, John, 85 n. 3

Palladius, 85 n. 6
Pannenberg, Wolfhart, 122
Patai, Raphael, 3, 9 n. 6, 38 n. 78
Pelikan, Jaroslav, 136 n. 7

Pesch, W., 86 n.12
Philo of Alexandria, 92
Pittenger, Norman, 53 n.7, 137 n.15
Plascow, Judith, 1, 8 n.2
Plato, 67 n.4
Polanyi, Michael, 40, 52 n.2
Prestige, G. L., 117 n.11, 135 n.1

Rahner, Karl, 38 n.78, 68 n.13, 87 n.26, 121, 135 n.2
Ramsey, Paul, 68 n.9
Rossi, Alice, 18
Russell, Gilbert, 20, 36 n.21
Russell, Letty, 4, 9 n.7, 17–19, 25–26, 31–32, 35 nn.16–18, 37 nn.42–44, nn.68–74, 136 n.6
Ruether, Rosemary Radford, 3, 4, 9 nn.6, 7, 10 n.10, 19–20, 25, 32, 35, 36 nn.20, 40, 37 nn.41, 75, 38 nn.76–77, 85 nn.5, 7
Ryle, Gilbert, 46

Saiving, Valerie, 62–63, 68 n.12
Sarkissian, Karekin, 83, 87 n.23
Sawicki, Marianne, 9 n.7, 67 n.1, 137 n.20
Sayers, Dorothy L. 73, 85 n.4
Schelkle, Karl Hermann, 85 n.3
Schillebeeckx, Edward, 113, 119 n.46
Schleiermacher, Friedrich, 121
Schnackenberg, Rudolf, 118 n.25
Schweitzer, Albert, 91
Sellers, Robert, 87 n.24
Sholem, Gershom, 67 n.4, 135 n.5
Smart, Ninian, 9 n.8, 135 n.1
Sobrino, Jon, 69 n.15
Spiceland, James, 137 n.15
Stagg, Evelyn and Frank, 85 n.3
Starhawk (Miriam Simos), 8 n.2, 23, 36 nn.31–34
Stein, Edith, 68 n.11

Stendahl, Krister, 67 n.3
Stolnitz, Jerome, 10 n.11
Suchocki, Marjorie, 29, 37 nn.52, 54–56, 136 n.6, 137 n.15
Swidler, Leonard, 3, 9 n.6, 36 n.38, 67 n.3, 85 n.3, 135 n.5
Swift, Kate, 67 n.1
Sykes, Stephen, 135 n.3

Tavard, George, 85 n.3, 136 nn.9, 10
Taylor, John, 136 n.12
Teilhard de Chardin, Pierre, 53 n.7, 59, 68 n.7, 89, 110–12, 116 n.3, 118 n.42
Temple, William, 90, 116 n.5, 117 n.16
Thomas Aquinas, 46, 79, 117 n.20
Tillich, Paul, 69 n.16, 117 n.14
Trible, Phyllis, 3, 9 n.6, 24, 36 n.38, 38 n.78

Ulanov, Ann Bedford, 14–16, 18, 35 nn.9–13

Vischer, Lucas, 135 n.4

Wainwright, Geoffrey, 135 n.3
Wallace-Hadrill, D. S., 86 n.14
Wand, Sr. Benedicta, 118 n.28
Warner, Maria, 86 n.17
Washbourne, Penelope, 8 n.2, 14, 16, 50
Welsh, Claude, 135 n.1, 136 n.9
Whitehead, Alfred North, 53 n.7
Wilson-Kastner, Patricia, 36 n.23, 52 n.4, 69 n.17, 85 nn.7, 8, 87 n.25
Wolfson, Harry Austin, 86 n.9, 117 nn.9, 11, 135 n.1

Zikmund, Barbara Brown, 9 n.6

Index of Scripture References

Genesis
1:26–27—58
1:26–30—60
2:4—3:24—97

Psalms
22—105

Matthew
16:15–16—1, 123
27:45–50—105
28:28—113, 123

Mark
14:36—123
15:33–37—105

Luke
10:38–42—72

John
1:1–14—77, 92–93
1:1–18—91
12:32—99
16:7–11—112

19:34–37—103

Acts
1—2—113
2:4—123
2:22–34—107
4:33—107

Romans
5:12–15—79
5:15–21—109
8:18–25—98, 107, 114
12:4–8—58
16:1–3—73

1 Corinthians
1:17–31—99, 107
11:4—73
12:1–30—58
15:12–22—107, 109
15:20–23—79
15:27–28—110, 112
15:42–58—109

Galatians
3:28—73, 79

Ephesians
1:10—110
1:20–23—101, 110
2:5–10—91
2:13–18—99
4:4–16—58

Colossians
1:15–23—91, 94, 101, 110
2:15—101
3:12–15—58
3:18—73

1 Timothy
2:12—73

1 Peter
3:1–2—73

Revelation
5:6–10—99
22:13—110